# MANAGEMENT CONTRACTING

*A practice manual*

# MANAGEMENT CONTRACTING

## A practice manual

### DEARLE & HENDERSON
CHARTERED QUANTITY SURVEYORS

*London*
E & F.N. SPON

First published in 1988 by
E. & F.N. Spon Ltd
11 New Fetter Lane, London EC4P 4EE

© 1988 Dearle & Henderson

Printed in Great Britain by
J. W. Arrowsmith Ltd, Bristol

ISBN 0 419 14440 4

*British Library Cataloguing in Publication Data*

Dearle & Henderson *(Firm)*
    Management contracting: A practice manual.
    1. Building—Contracts and specifications
    —Great Britain
    I. Title
    692'.8'0941     TH425
    ISBN 0-419-14440-4

# Contents

# Preface

This manual has been prepared to consolidate various procedures used by quantity surveyors in management contracting arrangements. The procedures relate mainly to the role of consultant quantity surveyors, but the manual should be of interest to those in contracting organizations, employer organizations and research and academic institutions.

It could be held that a practice manual in any field of endeavour is a precarious venture. This is certainly so when the field of endeavour is subject to changing procedures and opinions. Management contracting falls into this category, and this manual can therefore only reflect current circumstances.

The arrangement continues to attract discussion and revision on matters concerning the duties and responsibilities of parties, the form of management contract, the position of sub- (or works) contractors, and so forth. The procedures described in this manual must therefore be reviewed in the light of future developments.

Although the manual is primarily aimed at project or lead surveyors, those in an assisting role should also find it of use. However, it is assumed that the reader has a reasonable background in the various functions connected with tendering procedures, estimating, forecasting, cost control and the settlement of final accounts.

It would be unrealistic for a manual to attempt to cover the many aspects of these functions. Instead, points have been highlighted where the use of a management contract requires an amendment to common practice or it is important for the quantity surveyor to be aware of some special requirement.

The manual is divided into three main parts:

PART ONE   *Management contracting and the quantity surveyor.*
PART TWO   *Selection procedures and documentation.*
PART THREE   *Financial management.*

A fourth part contains the appendices, which show sample contracts, forms and documents useful in management contracting.

# *Part One*

# MANAGEMENT CONTRACTING AND THE QUANTITY SURVEYOR

This section of the manual provides background information on management contracting, together with a general description of the role of the quantity surveyor. Definitions of some of the more common terms used in management contracting are included.

## 1.1  What is management contracting?

Although management contracting is relatively new in the UK (development having mainly occurred over the past 15 years), forms of this contractual arrangement have been widely used in other countries – particularly in North America – for a much longer period. The essence of the arrangement is that it seeks to separate the responsibility for *management* of available resources from the actual *construction*, by removing or reducing the risk element of the firm providing the management skills.

Several definitions of management contracting are used in the construction industry despite the good efforts of some to establish a common vocabulary or glossary of terms. For the purpose of this manual the following definitions have been used.

*Management contracting*
A general term used in the construction industry for any contractual arrangement that seeks to place a special emphasis on the management of the construction process and the progress of design information.

Probably the two most common methods of achieving this are:

*The management contract arrangement*
An arrangement in which a contractor is appointed to manage both the construction and progress of design of the project. The employer has an 'Agreement to Build' with the management contractor, usually with the sanction of liquidated damages for any delays caused by factors that are within the control of the management contractor. The client may select the design team which is to work with the management contractor, or may place responsibility for undertaking the design with the management contractor.

*The construction management arrangement*
This is an arrangement more widely employed in the USA. Although similar in many respects to the management contract, the main difference is that the contracts for the works are executed directly between the various contractors and the employer. The organization appointed as the construction manager in effect acts in the role of the employer's management arm, and does not usually accept a liability for liquidated damages for delay. The

construction manager will, of course, be liable for proper performance of its duties in matters connected with time and the avoidance of delay.

*Management fee*
This is a further title adopted by firms offering a management contracting service but unfortunately has connotations of early systems where there was an expectation that the management contractor would execute a substantial part of the works from its own resources. This situation rarely occurs now.

In practice, variations in these arrangements occur especially in the matters of design responsibility and the extent to which an overall price can be guaranteed. For the purposes of this manual we have assumed a situation whereby design consultants are appointed independently by the employer and no express provision is included to seek a guaranteed maximum price from the management contractor.

Under a management contracting arrangement the construction requirements are identified as defined parcels of work (or work packages) including temporary work and site facilities. Lump-sum competitive tenders are normally obtained for each parcel as the scheme proceeds. Some work parcels can be let on a cost-reimbursable basis if this is considered more appropriate. This is often the basis for several of the temporary works parcels and common user facilities (preliminaries), but again lump-sum tenders can be obtained for these items. Some arrangements require the management contractor to provide a lump-sum price for preliminaries. This, however, introduces an area of commercial conflict between the employer and the contractor, which can reduce the independent aspect of the activities provided by the management contractor.

The costs of all work parcels are controlled within a budget to which the design team and management contractor are committed, and this is usually referred to as the Estimate of Prime Cost (EPC). Organizations offering the service of management contractor are usually building and civil engineering contractors. Construction management services are not confined to contractors, as other organizations including consortia of professional consultants and multidisciplinary practices also offer this service.

Although a variety of names are given to management contract arrangements, a large measure of commonality exists. This manual has concentrated on the common features rather than entering into the many theoretical distinctions. Of those identified above, the management contract arrangement is probably most commonly employed currently in the UK, so this manual concentrates on this form.

## 1.2  When to use management contracting

The management contract arrangement is one of several available to construction clients for procuring a construction project. As with any arrangement, the management contract must be assessed in terms of its suitability to meet the particular objectives of the employer and the circumstances of the project.

The following situations are particularly suitable for the use of the arrangement:

(1) When insufficient time or definition is available for the use of traditional methods which require a scheme to have reached an advanced stage of design before lump-sum tenders for the whole scheme are invited.

(2) When there is a need to demonstrate an early start to the construction phase which, with well-planned overlapping of design and construction, should also produce an early completion.

(3) When the complexity of the project demands that the management expertise of a construction organization is required on a low-risk basis in order to harness that expertise for the maximum benefit of the employer; for example assessing the 'buildability' or the economy of resources.

There are, of course, other circumstances which, taken separately, may not warrant the use of a management contract arrangement but in combination make it the most appropriate method.

## 1.3  The principal features of the management contract

In the absence of industry-wide model conditions of contract and standard forms of tender documentation (the Joint Contracts Tribunal Form having been only recently published) it is not surprising that the roles and relationships of the various parties to a management contract differ from scheme to scheme. It will be useful here to explain some of the principal features of a management contract, and how it differs from other forms of contract.

The arrangement seeks to obtain management expertise from a suitable organization on the basis of a low-risk agreement similar to that of other professionals on a project. In return for obtaining this expertise the employer pays a fee, usually based on the value of the works (or some defined adjusted value of the works), in a similar way to other professionals. As an alternative, in appropriate circumstances a lump-sum fee can also be agreed. When advised of this separate fee the initial reaction of many employers is to think they are paying a premium for this expertise. However, it must be stressed that this expertise and its cost are present in every form of contractual arrangement. It is only in the management contract (or arrangements similar to it) that this expertise is identified in the form of an independent service on behalf of the employer and attracts a separate fee.

### 1.3.1  *Avoidance of conflict within a management contract agreement*

There is much debate within the industry concerning the extent to which commercial conflict should be minimized within a management contract. In some quarters contracts are arranged which involve the contractor being paid a fee for some work and earning a profit for other work on the same scheme. In other quarters contracts are organized to ensure that the contractor is prevented from being paid anything other than a fee. It could be claimed that the latter approach enables the maximum benefit of the arrangement to be obtained by the employer since, conversely, any arrangement which sets up a commercial conflict between the management contractor and the employer could lead to the management contractor tempering advice in areas where the management contractor stood to earn a profit (or greater profit).

However, there are instances where it is preferable for the management contractor's direct resources to be employed on the works (e.g. in cases where resources need to be fully analysed). Here it should be possible to quantify the extent of the work involved and agree a fixed return on the resources employed.

Some employers prefer to enlarge the area for price competition by asking management contractors to offer a lump sum for site-based preliminaries. Such a lump sum is usually subject to adjustment for factors outside the control of the management contractor, but over-restrictive conditions will again lead to a mixed situation of the management contractor achieving low risk for some elements of cost and high risk for others.

To overcome the problems associated with conflict it is essential to develop a Management Contract Agreement which encourages a totally professional relationship between employer and management contractor. The agreement should be worded to produce a framework of professional intention. In some areas procedures can be described in detail, but these should be limited to the principal points of the agreement such as insurance, payments and damages. However, other areas can be left to be decided by the project team on the understanding that the most appropriate professional method will be employed. In essence such an agreement would resemble the conditions of engagement offered by a professional consultant, rather than a wordy and procedural form of contract associated with most other contractual arrangements.

A framework for a Management Contract Agreement is given in Appendix A. This framework has been used regularly by the authors and, when tailored for a particular scheme, is representative of the type of agreement that seeks to promote non-adversarial relationships.

### 1.3.2  *Implications of management contracts on the roles of the parties*

In most management contracts there is a tendency to shuffle or amend the conventional duties of the parties to the contract rather than producing any fundamental redefinition. For some employers the changed roles appear confusing and occasionally lead to the suggestion that duplication is involved.

This can be avoided when the management contractor is appointed early in the process and in sufficient time for a proper management system to be developed. The main implications of the arrangement on the roles of the parties are the following.

### (a)  Employer (client)

The employer must be in a position to respond quickly to the demands of the management contract process. This is especially important if the maximum benefit from overlapping the design and construction phases is to be obtained. In general the employer (or more especially the project manager) should expect to play a wide role in the approval and guidance aspects of the scheme, and employers should be made fully aware from the outset that this demand will be made on their time.

## (b) Design consultants

Design consultants will retain many of the duties and functions found under conventional arrangements, but in some management contracts there is a tendency to separate the responsibility for quality control. Except in cases where design and management is obtained from the management contractor, it is unlikely that design consultants will wish to see any part of the responsibility for quality control removed from their jurisdiction. Some design consultants may go further and consider it essential that they are given the responsibility for quality control, it becoming almost a condition precedent to accepting and fulfilling their design responsibility.

Equally, however, management contractors will claim that in order to carry out their responsibility for co-ordinating and managing the various contractors an element of quality control will be involved.

## (c) Consultant quantity surveyor

The consultant quantity surveyor's principal duty to the employer of providing overall financial control services will not be significantly amended under the management contract arrangement. However, several technical functions within that duty may be allocated to the management contractor. Most management contracts require the management contractor to prepare and take joint responsibility with the quantity surveyor for the accuracy of the EPC. Usually the management contractor will be asked to take responsibility for maintaining construction costs within the agreed EPC, but this is often a joint consultative process between the consultant quantity surveyor and the management contractor. Similar sharing of technical functions will be found in all aspects of the consultant quantity surveyor's role under the management contract. This is discussed in more detail later.

### (d) Management contractor

The management contractor's main role is to manage the construction and design progress of the project, including supervision of the works on site. Although the construction supervision role is well-understood by construction professionals, the role of managing design progress can vary from one scheme to another. To be effective the management contractor must be given authority, as well as responsibility, to progress the efficient flow of information from the design team to the construction team. This usually means that some of the design professionals have to accept a reduction in their customary role of project leader.

### 1.3.3 *Payments/retention provisions*

The basis of the reimbursement of costs under a management contract varies from scheme to scheme. If the scheme employs a relatively low-risk appointment for the management contractor, then payments to the management contractor will be largely of a cost-reimbursable type. The cost reimbursement will consist of two elements.

(1) Payments due under various work parcel contracts. These are usually lump-sum prices, but might in appropriate circumstances be cost reimbursable (or a combination).
(2) Payments to the management contractor for directly employed resources (usually site management and facilities costs, but may also include some of the permanent works).

In addition to the reimbursement of costs, the management contractor will be paid a fee. This fee may be a percentage of the value of (1) and (2) above or may be expressed in terms of a lump sum. Retention provisions will be developed to suit the particular circumstances of the scheme, but two distinct situations arise.

First, the principle of retention (if any) to be held against the management contractor will need to be resolved. It is customary for the fee to be paid monthly (in line with payments to works contractors), and some employers prefer the practice of holding retention. This corresponds to the situation of other professionals who are frequently paid in arrears.

Secondly, retentions to be held against work-parcel contractors will be based on conventional practice. In construction management arrangements where contracts are executed directly between employer and contractor, the employer will retain direct in accordance with the provisions of the contract. In management contracts retention will be held by the management contractor (with whom work-parcel contracts are executed). However, it is common practice for the management contractor to pass on the benefit of such retentions to the employer, and hence in practice the employer will hold retentions on both management contractor and work-parcel contractors.

### 1.3.4 *Damages for non-completion on time*

The management contractor offes to organize and manage the works to achieve a completed project within an agreed time and for or within the agreed EPC. In management contracts damages for non-completion on time may be organized in a similar way to that found under conventional contracts.

Not all management contracts use this conventional method; instead some limit the management contractor's liability for damages to those that the management contractor can obtain from the various work-parcel contractors who have actually caused the delay. (It should be noted that the management contractor will, of course, be liable for damages caused by events within the organization's control.) However, when this method is adopted a contractual problem arises, since work-parcel contractors may claim that the management contractor has in fact suffered no damages, and hence cannot be entitled to recover such damages.

To avoid this potential problem a method adopted in many forms of management contract is to impose liquidated and ascertained damages on the management contractor in the conventional manner. In turn the management contractor imposes a similar condition on each of the work-parcel contractors, but will usually adjust the damages figure on the basis of the value of the work parcel and status of the contractor. This is the method included in the suggested form of management contract contained in Appendix A.

### 1.3.5 *Absence of overall tender sum when construction commences*

Some employers are uneasy about this aspect of a management contract, especially those in the public sector where most standing orders have been developed for conventional contracts and have not been amended for the requirements of management contracts.

However, employers should be reassured that the absence of an overall tender sum at the commencement of construction does not necessarily mean a greater risk for the eventual construction costs. In fact, for some schemes it has been argued that tighter cost control is available under the arrangement, and hence greater assurance can be given to the matter of overall construction costs. Ultimately, assurance on costs at the commencement of construction can only be gauged by comparing the EPC with the circumstances of the scheme, and in particular design advancement, complexity, the site management framework, and so forth.

### 1.3.6 *Delays/Loss and expense*

With conventional lump-sum contracts the main contractor and domestic subcontractors are considered a single organization for most aspects of contractual liability. This fairly simple concept, although amended when nominations are involved, applies to the liability for delays and associated loss and expense.

Under the management contract the liability for delays and attendant loss and expense is more complex. The management contractor will not be held liable for delays that are caused by reasons outside the management contractor's reasonable control. Although in broad terms this is the same philosophy found in most standard forms of conventional contract under management contracts the management contractor will not be liable for delays caused by the various work-parcel contractors. Equally, each work-parcel contractor will not be eager to admit liability for delay or disruption.

This complexity sometimes leads to the criticism that the management contract arrangement is less stringent in its control over time than conventional contracts. However, this need not be – and rarely is – the case. The management contractor should be able to organize the works so as to offset and avoid many of the causes of delays. The project team, which includes the management contractor, must monitor closely the occurrence of delay or disruption in order to allocate the cause accurately and to ensure that the employer does not bear the costs of loss and expense which are more properly attributable to others.

### 1.3.7 *Damage to the works/injury to persons and property/insurances*

Management contracts should define clearly the responsibility for damage and injury and the insurances required to back up these responsibilities, especially where the management contractor is required to indemnify the employer.

The employer's requirements must be obtained when formulating or advising on contract procedures relating to these matters. For example, when working in existing properties it should be clearly established which party is responsible for damage to the properties by reason of special perils such as fire. Equally, when properties remain in occupation or a third party's possessions remain in the property during the execution of the works, the responsibility for insurance against damage to contents should be clearly established.

When the extent of the insurance to be taken up by the management contractor has been determined, the quantity surveyor will need to be aware of the financial implication of the 'excess' associated with each policy of the selected management contractor. Under a low-risk appointment the management contractor will seek reimbursement of any 'excess' where insurance is taken out to cover damage caused by special perils and the like. It can be arranged, of course, that a condition of the contract is that such excess will be borne by the management contractor.

Table 1 gives a checklist of the more common features of damage, injury and insurance matters related to conventional contracts. This can be used in connection with management contracts as an aid to establishing requirements.

### 1.3.8 *Contingency sums*

The very nature of construction sensibly demands that every contract should include a contingency sum to allow for unforeseen circumstances. The provision of contingency sums varies from

**Table 1** Provisions for injury, damage and insurance under building contracts

| Classifications commonly used in building contracts | Usual allocation of liability under contract | Usual insurance requirements | Remarks |
|---|---|---|---|
| 1. Injury to or death of any person caused by the carrying out of the works but *excluding* that caused by negligence of the employer (or persons for whom the employer is responsible) | Principal contractor is liable (plus cross-liability with subcontractors, etc.).<br><br>Standard forms usually require the principal contractor to indemnify the employer from the costs of any legal proceedings in connection with this classification of injury etc. (e.g. JCT SF80* clause 20.1) | To back up (but not to replace) indemnity most contracts require insurance to be taken out by the contractor (plus subcontractors) (e.g. JCT SF80* clause 21) | Open clauses of standard forms place a general liability on the contractor to carry out the works. This will automatically cover remedying defective work<br><br>Contractor's liability here extends only to contractor's own (plus subcontractor's, etc.) negligence. This is different from 1, above |
| 2. Injury or damage to any property arising from the carrying out of the works and caused by the contractor's negligence (contractor usually deemed to include subcontractors, servants and agents) but excluding injury and damage caused by special perils (fire, etc.) for which the employer is responsible | Principal contractor liable (plus cross-liability with subcontractors, etc.)<br><br>Above note on indemnity applicable here | As noted above | There exists a gap in the insurance cover when the standard forms of contracts are examined closely. Under 1, where neither party is negligent the contractor is liable. Under 2, where neither party is negligent the employer is liable. In both cases some of these 'blameless acts' are covered by insurance under 3, but this insurance normally applies to adjoining property and not the contract works |

| | | | |
|---|---|---|---|
| 3. Injury and damage caused by events that are often referred to as 'blameless acts', i.e. not caused by anyone's negligence | Employer liable | Most standard forms require contractor to insure (in joint names of contractor and employer) for damage caused by certain specific occurrences within this classification. This insurance usually attracts several exclusions (most familiar example is probably JCT 80* 21.2.1) and is limited to specified amounts for each event | Situation (b) rarely desirable. Insurance under (c) should include contents of occupiers (Note. In multi-occupier situations employers should ascertain what insurance provisions have been obtained by tenants)<br><br>In special circumstances insurance for existing structures can be taken out by contractor |
| 4. Injury and damage to the works caused by special perils (fire, etc.) | Contractor liable for loss. Opening clause of contract plus indemnity clauses such as JCT SF80* 20.1 establishes liability. When employer accepts responsibility for insuring works against special perils liability for such damage excluded from contractor's liability | Provisions for insurance of the works against special perils in most contracts covers three situations. Insurance for:<br><br>(a) New structures by contractors;<br>(b) New structures by employer;<br>(c) Existing structures by employer<br><br>Note. Also cover might be obtainable for liquidated and ascertained damages consequent upon extension of time granted in connection with the occurrence of special perils (e.g. JCT SF80* 22D) | |
| 5. Excepted risks – nuclear perils | Employer liable, but in the case of damage caused by aerial pressure waves the contractor may still have an obligation to complete under general duty expressed in opening clause of contract (unlikely to be enforceable, however) | Damage arising from nuclear activities are rarely insurable, and damage from aerial pressure waves are uninsurable. Therefore no contractual requirement | |
| | | *General*<br>Contractor's liabilities above are often covered by an 'all risks' type insurance policy. Policy should be in joint names and cover all risks except those stated (e.g. in line with JCT SF80* Clause 22A) | |

JCT SF80 Standard Form of Building Contract 1980 Edition, published by the Joint Contracts Tribunal.

scheme to scheme. Some employers include allowances within the contract documents; others make provision outside the contract.

The selection of the management contract arrangement invariably means that the design for many elements of the scheme is at an early stage when the management contractor is formally appointed. Additionally, the interface on site of a large number of contractors contractually independent of each other can lead to increased expenditure for the employer where liability for damage cannot be reasonably allocated to other parties.

These factors should persuade employers to maintain a larger contingency at the commencement of the contract than they perhaps would under conventional contracts. As the design and tendering phases of the scheme develop, the degree of uncertainty reduces and a more precise view can be taken of the level of contingencies to be maintained for the remainder of the contract.

### 1.3.9 *Phases of a management contract*

Conventional contracts have two distinct stages or periods: precontract and post-contract. The appointment of the principal or main contractor is usually the dividing point.

The management contract arrangement does not fit so neatly into the conventional pattern, but usually three distinct periods can be identified.

(1)  Period before the appointment of the management contractor.
(2)  Preconstruction period.
(3)  Construction period.

Period (1) will contain many of the actions associated with conventional precontract phases, but will usually be on an accelerated timescale.

The appointment of the management contractor will see the commencement of the preconstruction period (period 2). This is usually relatively short, because the ability to overlap design and construction under a management contract facilitates an early commencement of site operations. This period is usually taken up with identifying critical activities and items, ordering long lead items, firming up the programme, agreeing a contract EPC and establishing the management framework and routines for the remainder of the contract.

The third period is self-explanatory and will also include the period for the settlement of any matters when construction is complete.

## 1.4 The quantity surveyor's role

### 1.4.1 *The period before the appointment of the management contractor*

The quantity surveyor's role and duties will be very similar to those found under conventional contracts and will, of course, be dependent on how early the quantity surveyor is brought into the 'project management' team.

Management contracting is only one of several methods of procurement that can be employed, and it is frequently the quantity surveyor who is asked to identify the circumstances in a scheme that might make management contracting most suitable. The quantity surveyor must give prudent advice, and ensure that other members of the design team – especially the leading design consultants – are aware of the implications on their roles. The architect or supervising officer in particular will be asked to accept the fact that the management of the flow of information from designer to the site will be controlled by the management contractor, and this may be seen by lead designers as diminishing their team leader role.

During this period the quantity surveyor will also be involved in the more conventional financial duties, such as estimating, cost planning, consideration of construction-related tax allowances, life-cycle costs, and so forth.

Once the decision to proceed with a management contract arrangement has been taken, it is necessary to organize the selection of the management contractor. The work of the quantity surveyor in this process is fully described in Part Two of this manual.

### 1.4.2 *The preconstruction period*

As mentioned earlier, preconstruction periods in management contract arrangements are usually quite short, since the arrangement has usually been adopted to enable work to commence on site quickly. However, sufficient time must be available for certain procedures within the management system to be developed before the physical works begin. The quantity surveyor's work during this period is usually described in the management contract or the contractor's submission document accompanying the contract. The principal tasks are the following.

## (a) Development and agreement of the EPC

Whether initially provided by the management contractor or the quantity surveyor, most management contracts require that the budget EPC or cost plan will be developed into an agreed EPC which will then be incorporated in the formal contract document. In the short time available during this period it is common for the budget EPC to be adjusted only for the purposes of reallocating certain items of work or refining figures in the light of better information. (For example, from preliminary tender enquiries submitted by works contractors.) Similarly, any changes to the scope of the works that are requested by the employer can be incorporated.

At the end of this process the quantity surveyor and the management contractor should be able to agree that the contract EPC provides a realistic budget within which to control the costs of the project. In many respects the EPC can be considered in the same light as a cost plan based on a similar level of information, in other words a control tool.

## (b) Development and agreement of contract procedures

It is unlikely that a management contract will introduce any fundamentally new procedures or functions. However, the tasks associated with these procedures are frequently allocated in a manner not found under conventional contracts. For example, although the system of lump-sum competitive tendering is widely understood, when using the management contract the task of producing various documents and performing certain tasks by agreed dates may be distributed in an unfamiliar way. It is therefore essential that the detailed tasks of all procedures be clearly allocated during the preconstruction period, based upon the duties shown in the initial enquiry document. The management contract will contain definitions in broad terms of the principal responsibilities, but it cannot pinpoint every task. The quantity surveyor will be particularly concerned during this stage with the proposed methods of budgetary control and accounting, the manner in which the management contractor proposes to maintain cost and contractual records, the financial information and the arrangements for producing statements required by the project team and the employer.

Other members of the project team will scrutinize the management arrangements that impact on their own performance. Consultants responsible for design aspects will be concerned with the programme for information flow and arrangements for quality control.

The quantity surveyor will also be involved and will participate in the development of programmes for procurement and construction, even though the management contractor will play the leading part. The quantity surveyor can make an invaluable contribution during this stage advising on any employer's requirements or standing orders that may need to be included within any procedures and programme.

## 1.4.3  *The construction period*

During this period procedures established during preconstruction will be maintained, and any that are outstanding will be developed. It will be appreciated that many of the tasks performed by the quantity surveyor during this period are similar to conventional post-contract services. However, due to the overlapping of design, tendering and construction, the quantity surveyor will be involved in a greater number of technical functions at any one time than in the conventional post-contract phase.

It should be noted that most management contracts generate a large number of work parcels. Many schemes generate more than 50 work parcels, and some more than 100. It is essential that the members of the team providing information for the procurement of the work parcels perform within the programmed timescales.

From the quantity surveyor's point of view, especially where the quantity surveyor is responsible for the preparation of tendering documentation the use of standard documents, backed up by modern word-processing facilities, can be a key to the successful implementation of the procurement and construction programme. Although the work is technically demanding, its success is more dependent on the management of the paper flow through the system than any other factor.

Overall, the quantity surveyor's principal task is the financial administration of the contract. It is here that the quantity surveyor will notice an increased intensity in his role. Although basic skills of estimating and forecasting will be largely unamended from those used in conventional arrangements, the cost monitoring and reporting systems will need to accommodate the special requirements of management contracts. These aspects are discussed in detail in Part Three of this manual. It also describes in detail a budgetary and accounting system developed by the authors for use on management contracts.

# Part Two

---

# SELECTION PROCEDURES AND DOCUMENTATION

---

This section covers a suggested procedure and documentation for the selection of the management contractor. Reference has also been made to the selection of work-parcel contractors, although on most schemes this is a joint process between the quantity surveyor and the management contractor.

## 2.1  Selecting a management contractor

Unlike conventional tendering, the industry has not developed any nationally agreed codified procedure for management contract tendering: several procedures are employed. The procedure described below has been developed in the light of experience gained over the past 15 years on a variety of different schemes.

The procedure is organized into stages as follows:

Stage 1 – Preliminary list.
Stage 2 – Short list.
Stage 3 – Formal tender enquiry.
Stage 4 – Evaluation.
Stage 5 – Final selection.

### 2.1.1  *Stage 1 – Preliminary list*

This stage resembles the preliminary list stage of conventional tendering. Usually no more than 10 management contractors would be examined at this stage. The contractors would be assessed by the project team and employer on the basis of reputation, experience and capability to undertake the work.

### 2.1.2  *Stage 2 – Short list*

In view of the sometimes large amounts of work undertaken by management contractors in tendering, it is advisable that a short list of only between four and six proceed to the formal tender stage. The fairest and usually most efficient way of assessing short-list candidates is the holding of interviews at which the employer and the project team can explain the project and ask relevant questions of the management contractor to assess the management contractor's attitude to the scheme envisaged.

In order to streamline the interview process it is advisable to send out a brief description of the project and the employer's objectives together with a preliminary agenda for the interview. In this way contractors can organize their team and information so as to communicate more effectively the principal features of their organizations.

At this stage the employer and project team, on the basis that the contractor wants to undertake the project, will be looking for satisfactory answers to the following.

(1) Has the contractor sufficient experience of management contracting?
(2) Has the contractor a separate organization for management contracting, and what relationship does it have with the parent company?
(3) Has the contractor the necessary specific experience for the project under consideration?
(4) What are the management, technical and financial resources of the company available to work on the project?

At the interview the opportunity should be taken to outline the preconstruction programme. The management contractor should also be told as precisely as possible what will be required in the submission accompanying his formal tender.

It is good practice to record the results of the short-listing stage formally, and in some cases it may be a requirement to report to the employer for approval. Sometimes project teams find comparative or score sheets useful in framing decisions.

### 2.1.3  Stage 3 – Formal tender enquiry

The term 'formal tender enquiry' is used for the formal submission stage of the selection process. The word 'tender' is more commonly associated with the competitive price process which forms part of conventional contractual arrangements. When using the management contract the competitive pricing elements are usually confined to the management fee. However, competition on service and facilities is just as important as the management fee.

The project team should provide the management contractor with as much information as possible. This includes clearly demonstrating the level of design so far achieved, and any lack of information on the scheme. In this way the management contractor will be encouraged to prepare a very open submission outlining the areas requiring greatest input. Any attempt to conceal the current true nature of the evolution of the scheme will only lead to misunderstandings and an incorrect relationship between the management contractor and the rest of the team.

No matter how scant the information available, this should be embodied into a formal set of documents with a clear statement of what the management contractor is to provide in support of a tender. It is advisable for the team to produce a submission framework into which the management contractor is directed to provide information in a uniform manner. This has the added advantage of speeding up the evaluation stage.

Constructive suggestions from the management contractor should be encouraged at this stage, and the tender enquiry documents should allow the submission of alternatives. It is customary for the formal tender documents to contain the following sections.

(1) A general description of the works and all known site and operational restrictions in a similar manner to that used for conventional preliminaries.

(2) A statement of the duties and responsibilities of the parties in both the preconstruction and the construction periods. A typical example of this section is included in Appendix B.

(3) A specification and quantitative document or framework to aid the contractor in preparation (or in some cases confirmation) of the EPC.

(4) Programme requirements and constraints.

(5) A definition of the items to be included in the management fee. An example of this definition is included in the Form of Agreement (Appendix A).

(6) Definition of prime cost. An example is included in the Form of Agreement (Appendix A).

(7) A copy or details of the Management Contract–Building Agreement. Normally the Form of Contract should be prepared by the employer but situations do exist whereby the contractor is asked to submit a preferred form. The form included in Appendix A is a suitable basis for employer-prepared forms. The Joint Contracts Tribunal has recently published Articles of Agreement and Conditions for use in management contracts.

The above document will, of course, be accompanied by a formal letter of invitation, instructions for tenderers and all relevant drawings.

Although the items listed above are self-explanatory (especially by reference to the various Appendices provided) it is perhaps worthwhile discussing item 3 further. This has been termed 'Specification and Quantitative Document or Framework'.

The format and content of this document will vary from scheme to scheme, depending on the extent of the information available and the extent to which the project team are required to provide such information. Specification data can be obtained from design consultants, and where drawings are scant a broad quantitative framework can be prepared to assist the contractor in assessing the resources required for the project.

Where the management contractor is required to prepare the EPC, the tender enquiry will make it clear that the quantitative document is indicative and is to be used as a guide.

In the past some management contractors treated the quantitative document in the same way as a conventional Bill of Quantities, where in effect the employer guarantees the correctness of the document. Experienced management contractors now accept the true role of this quantitative document.

### 2.1.4 *Stage 4 – Evaluation*

It is essential to prepare a detailed evaluation of the contractors' tender submissions before inviting them to participate further in the selection process. The detailed evaluation will, of course, reflect the priorities of the scheme, but some common areas exist in all schemes. These are discussed briefly and include:

(a) Financial assessment;
(b) Programme;
(c) Method statement;
(d) Management/organization;
(e) Personnel;
(f) Other considerations.

### (a) Financial assessment

Most management contracts require that the EPC be agreed between the management contractor and the quantity surveyor before the signing of the contract. The quantity surveyor will therefore be concerned with evaluating tenders in order to assess what adjustments will have to be made to the submitted EPC. This will involve analysing rates for labour and other contractor-owned resources intended to be employed in the scheme concentrating on standard-hour weeks, bonus expectations and similar matters. The reliability of budget estimates for work-parcel tenders and the level of contingency in relation to the extent of design completed will also need to be assessed.

Site preliminaries costs and associated management that are to be reimbursed on a cost basis will need to be checked for adequacy. In particular, time-related costs will need to be judged in relation to the overall submitted programme, since there is a tendency for the submitted preliminaries cost to be on the low side in order to make the total EPC appear attractive to the employer.

The management fee will need to be viewed against the contractor's statement of what the fee will cover. There is a tendency for employers to become excessively concerned with the percentage quotations, rather than what is being provided and how credible the offer is. The percentage is a good guide to the quality of service, but analysis of what is included for site personnel/head office personnel will partly explain why there are variations in percentages. (It should be noted that under most management contracts site-based personnel are reimbursable whereas head office personnel are covered by the fee.)

## (b)  Programme

The management contractor will be asked to submit both preconstruction and construction programmes. There is a tendency for many management contractors to assume that a short preconstruction programme is an essential objective of the employer. In some cases this may be true, but it has to be realistic and provide sufficient time for decisions and evaluations to be made by the employer and his team. This factor, often overlooked by management contractors, requires special attention during the evaluation. The programme will also affect the time-related cost elements of the scheme, and any possible adjustments to a contractor's programme must be evaluated and included in the financial assessment.

## (c)  Method statement

Most management contract enquiries are produced in advance of detailed design proposals. Hence, forms of construction and their method of execution are rarely comprehensively established. It is therefore essential to obtain a statement of the management contractor's methods of executing and organizing the works. This factor is particularly important in refurbishment schemes, especially where tenants are to remain in occupation. In such cases careful examination will need to be made of the contractor's proposed methods for minimizing disruption, noise and dust, and providing satisfactory environmental conditions for the tenants.

## (d) Management/organization

This heading covers many aspects associated with construction management, tendering procedures, arrangements for cost control, site security, emergency repairs, and so forth.

The quantity surveyor in particular will wish to be assured of the soundness of the contractor's proposals for tendering and cost control of the work parcels, and how they harmonize with the quantity surveyor's own methods.

## (e) Personnel

It is essential that the employer should be able to identify and assess the quality of the personnel who will be directly responsible for the various aspects of the scheme. In keeping with most modern commercial organizations those attending interviews or making presentations are not necessarily those who will take an active part in the project.

Some management contractors appoint their own teams of consultants, especially for design services. It is essential that a statement is obtained from the contractor, indicating the nature and extent of all contracts given to consultants.

Finally, for key personnel such as the site manager, assurances must be obtained from the contractor that other commitments will not jeopardize the effectiveness of such key personnel. Rarely will good staff be idle when a new project occurs, but the management contractor will need to demonstrate that planned resources will be sufficiently free at the appropriate time.

## (f) Other considerations

Other aspects of the evaluation will include quality control, procedures for meetings, planning and building regulation matters. These matters will generally be of more relevance to other team members rather than to the quantity surveyor. However, any financial implications of adjustments made to these matters will need to be assessed by the quantity surveyor.

## 2.1.5 *Stage 5 – Final selection*

After the evaluation it is advisable and only courteous to provide each contractor with an opportunity to clarify or explain any matters or queries raised by the team during the evaluation process. Where the contractors' submissions are very similar, or where the contractor is contributing to and undertaking design, a final selection interview and presentation may be necessary.

It must be remembered that a true management contracting service is very similar to other professional services which are very dependent on the personalities involved. The final selection meeting or interview provides the opportunity to meet the individuals who will be responsible for certain aspects of the scheme.

It is advisable to provide an agenda for any final selection meetings, and sufficient time must be made available if the management contractor is to make a presentation. The query-and-answer session will form only part of the meeting.

It is essential that the employer be represented at any final selection interview or meeting, because the employer is ultimately responsible for the management contractor's appointment, even though the recommendation may come from the employer's project team. In this way the employer can establish the management contractor's attitude towards matters that affect the employer. Interview assessment sheets can be useful in recording major points, especially if interviews are arranged over a few days (do not trust memory). The criteria for selection will vary from scheme to scheme, and for this reason a 'standard' assessment sheet is not recommended. When the selection panel has reached agreement a formal report of the evaluation and selection will be made to the employer.

## 2.2  Work-parcel contract procedures

### 2.2.1  *Generally*

To maximize the benefits of a management contract it is essential that the majority of tendering and contractual arrangements for the work-parcel contracts are determined during the preconstruction period.

As noted earlier, the responsibilities of the management contractor and quantity surveyor will be slightly changed from conventional tendering procedures. Which party will be employed for the preparation of various aspects of the tendering and contractual documentation will need to be agreed if not already stated in the tender enquiry.

The common situation is for the contractor to submit names of proposed tenderers to the employer and project team for approval. Thereafter the management contractor is given responsibility for organizing the despatch and receipt of tender documents. The preparation of tender documents will usually be a joint effort between the quantity surveyor and management contractor. So, too, will be the evaluation of tenders, with contributions from others as appropriate.

An essential early task will be for the full range of work-parcel contracts to undergo an examination to establish which common items will be required in every tender. From this, standard forms and wording can be produced which with modern office aids will streamline the procurement process.

The common items are:

(1) General conditions (or preliminaries) including contract and insurance provisions;
(2) Dayworks provisions (but not necessarily the sums involved);
(3) General summary;
(4) Form of tender (amended for particular work-parcel contract);
(5) Site establishment information/plans, etc.;
(6) Overall programme.

The following items within each tender document will be specially written for each parcel:

(1) Special conditions. These will refer to special matters not covered under the general conditions.
(2) Descriptions of materials and workmanship. These will be trade preambles and/or specifications for the items of work contained in the work-parcel.
(3) Measured work/pricing document. This may range from SMM-based measurement to some form of pricing schedule (SMM, Standard method of measurement of building work).

(4) Restraints programme. This will indicate the programming requirements for each work-parcel contractor.

### 2.2.2 *Form of parcel/work-package contract*

Some management contractors have prepared their own 'in-house' forms of contract. Such forms should be examined to ensure that terms and conditions are customary within the industry and are no less favourable to the employer than terms found under standard forms of contract. Assessment will need to be made to ensure that the employer's interests are protected in matters of damages, reasons for extension of time, treatment of fluctuations, and so forth.

Some management contractors use amended versions of standard forms, and a copy of a typical example of this is included as Appendix C. Here it will be noted that the terms 'subcontract' and 'subcontractor' have been retained. These terms refer to the work-parcel contractor. In Appendix C the management contractor has used the Standard Form of Subcontract for use where a subcontractor is nominated under the Standard Form of Building Contract with appropriate amendments and additional clauses. In addition, for the operation of the parcel contract but for no other purpose, all reference to the main contract has been deemed to be a reference to the JCT Standard Form of Building Contract, but with a proviso that the Management Contract will override anything contained in the Standard Form. This arrangement provides a satisfactory administrative format, and saves the reproduction of clauses controlling payment, damages, and so forth.

The Joint Contracts Tribunal has published a Works Contract (ref. WC/1) for use in management contracts.

# Part Three

---

# FINANCIAL
# MANAGEMENT

---

This section examines the role of the quantity surveyor in financial management aspects of management contracting. The common functions of financial management are discussed under three broad headings:

(1) Budgetary control and accounting;
(2) Cost and productivity monitoring;
(3) Financial projections/studies.

The services provided under item (1) are required in some form for every management contract, and hence this section of the manual has concentrated in detail on the system developed for this purpose.

The extent to which quantity surveyors are involved in item (2) depends on the particular nature of the scheme. Some schemes for which management contracts are used require the economic viability of the management and construction resources to be tested. In such cases the management contractor's contribution to 'buildability' can only be truly measured by the adoption of work study and measurement techniques. This aspect of financial management is discussed under a separate heading later in this section of the manual.

The quantity surveyor's services provided under item (3) again differ from scheme to scheme, with the most common being the preparation of regular cash-flow projections. As management contracts are usually employed on complex schemes and can represent a greater uncertainty on costs for the employer than is found under conventional contracts, risk analysis is finding increasing usage. These aspects are discussed briefly.

It will be appreciated that although the text has divided the discussion, the work carried out under the three headings is interrelated. For example, studies into productivity will be used in forecasting future costs within the budgetary control system, and so forth.

## 3.1 Budgetary control and accounting

It is accepted that quantity surveyors' conventional cost control and final account systems and procedures can be employed to a large extent in management contracts. However, it is recognized that the management contract, due mainly to its number of separate work parcels within an accelerated timescale, places different demands on a quantity surveyor than are found under conventional contracts.

In terms of procedures and documentation the management contract in many ways resembles a conventional contract with an excessive number of nominations needing to be let during the construction period of the project. It is (or should be) rare for conventional contracts to have 50 or more major nominations, but with the management contract arrangement this is a normal number of parcels or work packages. Hence, a system is needed that enables the quantity surveyor to work effectively. The system described in the following has been developed to meet these needs and can be adopted (and where necessary adapted) for most management contracts.

### 3.1.1 *Basic features of the system*

The system has been designed to achieve two management objectives.

(1) An attempt has been made to avoid duplication of effort. To achieve this the system has integrated the documentation required for projecting final costs and settling the final accounts of the various work parcels.

(2) The system has been designed so as to lend itself to easy transference to currently available 'spreadsheet' computer applications. As with any system of management control, computer and manual applications can never completely harmonize in all respects. Therefore, when the system is used as a total manual application certain minor adjustments to the quantity surveyor's working must be made. However, these adjustments are minimal in nature and do not amend the basic organization behind the system.

The system is defined in a series of forms. A blank set of these forms is given in Appendix D, and they are summarized below.

Form 1 – Financial statement;
Form 2 – Summary of projected/final cost (two sheets);
Form 3 – Projected/final cost record sheet;
Form 4 – Projected/final cost collection sheet;
Form 5 – (Sub-)parcel reconciliations sheet (two sheets);
Form 6 – Accounting record sheet, cost reimbursable;
Form 7 – Expenditure review;
Form 8 – General-use materials record;
Form 9 – Quantity surveyor's Report, valuation (three sheets)

### 3.1.2  Operation of the system

#### (a)  The major forms: 1, 2, 3, 4 and 5

The budget for a management contract is usually based on the agreed EPC. The agreed EPC often represents the limit of approval given to the scheme by the employer, and in such circumstances this together with the management fee is the total authorization for construction costs. On top of this the employer will, of course, have allocated allowances for all other procurement costs (such as professional fees and land costs) including a contract contingency to be expended with the employer's approval. Alternatively the contingency may be retained and controlled by the employer outside the contract's financial arrangements.

The EPC will in turn have been allocated into work parcels including, where applicable, parcels of site management and facilities costs. Under arrangements which obtain a lump-sum quotation for preliminaries from the management contractor, the value of preliminaries will not be included in the EPC but will, of course, form part of the overall budget for the scheme.

At the centre of the system is the projected/final cost record sheet (form 3). This is provided for every work parcel. Often a parcel will consist entirely of the works of one contractor or occasionally the direct costs of the management contractor. In other cases the parcel may be divided between several contractors and the management contractor. In the latter case a form 3 will be allocated to each subparcel and all subparcels will be consolidated in a projected/final cost collection sheet (form 4). Before commencing a form 3 it will be necessary to carry out a once-and-for-all (sub-)parcel tender reconciliation. Form 5 has been produced to record this reconciliation, an example of which is shown in Fig. 1. The information shown in this example has been transferred to the example provided of a form 3 (Fig. 2).

Form 3 has been designed to provide an overall picture of the budgetary and cost situation at any given time for each work-parcel or subparcel. To support this sheet the quantity surveyor will use conventional cost-estimating and final account techniques and paperwork. A worked example of this form is shown in Fig. 2. Explanatory notes have been inserted as handwritten text and foot-notes. It will be useful to discuss further the treatment of fluctuations.

Some employers will set a total budget authorization within which the value of fluctuations must be contained. In the worked example the employer can approve additional expenditure for fluctuations, so these are separated from the contract costs in the manner shown. In the record sheet (form 3), for 'windows and screens', it will be noted that a total of £8000 is shown in fluctuations which consists of:

(1) £7000 from original tender (transferred from form 5);
(2) £500 from the rest of items 1–3;
(3) £500 as an allowance for any remaining.

The figures contained in each parcel record sheet (or in the case of several subparcels the figures contained in the collection sheet) are taken to the summary of projected/final costs (form 2) (Fig. 3). The information from this summary is transferred in a consolidated format to the financial report (form 1) (Fig. 4).

Forms 1 and 2 will be circulated to the employer and, where appropriate, other members of the team. Additional information can be provided in the form of purpose-designed appendices. Precise details of a project's financial report format should be obtained during the preconstruction period. If no separate approval for fluctuations is available, then items 3 and 8 of form 1 are not utilized.

It will be seen from the above that all figures from the parcel record sheet upwards eventually end up as a single total for the scheme. It will therefore be appreciated how the computerization of this system assists the surveyor. In essence the computer system removes the necessity to transfer the figures physically, since any single alteration to any one record sheet is automatically transferred by the computer through the other forms to the financial report. This is particularly important since the agreement of final accounts for the various work parcels will occur at irregular intervals during the whole of the construction phase (as well as after construction). Hence, the budgetary control report will be an amalgam of estimated and actual final costs.

```
(SUB) PARCEL RECONCILIATION SHEET (1)

CONTRACT: BLANK REDEVELOPMENT BLANKSHIRE              JOB NO: 5000


PARCEL REF: 23 WINDOWS AND SCREENS
            ACE WINDOWS LTD
                                                              £

ACCEPTED TENDER (Exclusive of cash discount) ..........   156650.00

Deduct Contingencies and Dayworks ....................      4500.00


                              Balance ...........       152 150.00

CONTRACT EPC .........................................   150 000.00


                    Amount of Accepted Tender
                    Above/below Contract EPC             2150.00  ❶



Value/Assessment of Fluctuations
contained in Accepted Tender                         £    7000.00


Value of items contained in amount of
Accepted Tender above/below Contract
EPC that will not be included in Final
Adjusted EPC                                         £    2150.00

Brief Description           £
                          + or  (-)




                        NIL                              —
                                          Less
Non-EPC Adj.            NIL                Adj. EPC      2150.00
```

❶ This figure taken to form 3 (refer A1 29).

**Fig. 1** (Form 5, sheet 1)

| (SUB) PARCEL RECONCILIATION SHEET (2) | | PARCEL REF 23 |
| CONTRACT : BLANK REDEVELOPMENT BLANKSHIRE | | JOB NR : 5000 |
| List of Provisional Sums contained in tender (other than Contingencies and Dayworks) | | SUB-PARCEL - ACE WINDOWS LTD |

| Ref | Description | Amount £ |
| --- | --- | --- |
| – NIL – | NIL | NIL |

**Fig. 1** (Form 5, sheet 2)

PROJECTED/FINAL COST RECORD SHEET

WORK PARCEL REF **23 WINDOWS AND SCREENS**  CONTRACT **BLANK REDEVELOPMENT BLANKSHIRE**

JOB NO: **5000**

SUB PARCEL REF **ACE WINDOWS LTD.**

1. CONTRACT EFC

❶ A. Cost reimbursable allocation
   B. Fixed-price allocation

| | A £ | B £ |
|---|---|---|
| | | 150 000.00 |

2. ESTIMATED VALUE OF A/SO INSTRUCTIONS

❷

| A/SO/I No | Non-EFC Adj A £ | Non-EFC Adj B £ | Adj EFC A £ | Adj EFC B £ | A £ | B £ |
|---|---|---|---|---|---|---|
| 29 PLACE SUB-CONTRACT | - | - | - | 2150 | | |
| 36 AMEND GLASS NORTH WING | - | - | - | 4500 | | |
| 43 OMIT W/IN LOCKS W/IN 57.99 | - | - | - | (3000) | | |
| 50 EMERGENCY WK. (LATE ORDER) | - | 1000 | - | - | | |
| C/Fwd | - | 1000 | - | 3650 | - | 150 000.00 |

2. CON'T

| A/SO/I No: | Non-EFC Adj A £ | Non-EFC Adj B £ | Adj EFC A £ | Adj EFC B £ | A £ | B £ |
|---|---|---|---|---|---|---|
| B/FWD | - | 1000 | - | 3650 | | |
| | | | | | | |
| ADJUSTED EFC | //// | 1000 | - | 3650 | - | 153650.00 |
| | | | | | | 1000.00 |
| | | | | | | 154650.00 ❺ |

3. OTHER ADJUSTMENTS

| | A £ | B £ |
|---|---|---|
| (a) EXTRA W/W'S WEST WING – (AI AWAITED) | | 2000 |
| (b) POSSIBLE CLAIM FOR LATE ORDER BY MAIN CONTR. | | 2500 |
| | - | 4500.00 ❺ |

4. FLUCTUATIONS

(a) INCLUDED IN 1-3 ABOVE £7500 ......... 500.00
(b) ALLOWANCE FOR REMAINDER = £500 ......... 4000.00

5. CONTINGENCY (ORIGINAL SUB-CONTRACT CONTINGENCY £4500 NOW £4000)

PROJECTED/FINAL COST ......... 163650.00

| | A £ | B £ |
|---|---|---|
| | - | 163650.00 |

Notes:

❶ Columns A and B used as appropriate. Some sub-parcels might contain both allocations.

❷ This information obtained from sub-parcel reconciliation form.

❸ Items (a) and (b) include allowance for man. fee.

❹ If tender on fully fluctuating basis item 4 would be used to project total fluctuations.

❺ 1000 / 4500 / 5500 This figure taken to other adjustments box on form 4. Conventional A/C sheets used as back-up to all other A/SO/I's.

Fig. 2 (Form 3)

| CONTRACT: | BLANK REDEVELOPMENT, BLANKSHIRE FOR ACME DEVELOPMENTS LTD | | | | | | | JOB NO: 5000 |
|---|---|---|---|---|---|---|---|---|

**SUMMARY OF PROJECTED/FINAL COST:**   **FINANCIAL REPORT NO: 4**   **DATE: SEPTEMBER 1987**   **SHEET 1**

| WORK PARCEL | | CONTRACT EFC £ | PROJECTED FINAL COST £ | CONTAINED WITHIN PROJECTED FINAL COST | | | | REMARKS |
|---|---|---|---|---|---|---|---|---|
| No: | Title | | | FLUCTUATIONS £ | EFC ADJUSTMENTS £ | OTHER ADJUSTMENTS £ | CONTINGENCY £ | |
| 1 | Site Management | 200 000 | 210 000 | 10 000 | – | – | – | Covers A.I's 1.52 |
| 2 | General Duties Gang | 30 000 | 33 000 | 3 000 | – | – | – | |
| 3 | Safety/Welfare | 25 000 | 28 000 | 3 000 | – | – | – | |
| 4 | Site Security | 15 000 | 17 000 | 2 000 | – | – | – | |
| 5 | Site Accommodation | 60 000 | 72 000 | 12 000 | – | – | – | |
| 6 | Site Furniture | 5 000 | 10 000 | 1 000 | 4 000 | – | – | |
| 7 | Site Copier/Computer | 20 000 | 12 000 | – | (8 000) | – | – | |
| 8 | Telephones | 6 000 | 7 000 | 1 000 | – | – | – | |
| 9 | Scaffolding | 150 000 | 184 000 | 30 000 | – | – | 4 000 | |
| 10 | Plant | 250 000 | 280 000 | 30 000 | – | – | – | Includes add hoist |
| 11 | Temporary Services | 20 000 | 22 000 | 2 000 | – | – | – | |
| 12 | Temporary Roads | 10 000 | 4 000 | – | (6 000) | – | – | |
| 13 | Debris Disposal | 10 000 | 11 000 | 1 000 | – | – | – | |
| 14 | Insurances and Bond | 10 000 | 22 000 | – | 12 000 | – | – | |
| 15 | Sundry ❶ | 22 000 | 20 000 | 2 000 | (2 000) | – | – | |
| 16 | Excavation and Filling | 115 000 | 108 500 | – | (2 500) | – | 4 000 | |
| 17 | Sundry Earthworks | 15 000 | 4 518 | – | (10 482) | – | – | |
| | C/FWD | 963 000 | 1 045 018 | 97 000 | (12 982) | – | 8 000 | |

❶ This parcel used as a general 'dumping' item for sundries (eg. general use materials, petty cash etc.)

**Fig. 3** (Form 2, sheet 1)

CONTRACT: BLANK REDEVELOPMENT, BLANKSHIRE FOR ACME DEVELOPMENTS LTD — JOB NO: 5000

SUMMARY OF PROJECTED/FINAL COST: — FINANCIAL REPORT NO: 4 — DATE: SEPTEMBER 1987 — SHEET 2

| WORK PARCEL No: | Title | CONTRACT EFC £ | PROJECTED FINAL COST £ | CONTAINED WITHIN PROJECTED FINAL COST: | | | | REMARKS |
|---|---|---|---|---|---|---|---|---|
| | | | | FLUCTUATIONS £ | EFC ADJUSTMENTS £ | OTHER ADJUSTMENTS £ | CONTINGENCY £ | |
| | B/Fwd | 963 000 | 1 045 018 | 97 000 | (12 982) | – | 8 000 | |
| 18 | Concrete work in substructures drainage and road kerbs | 365 000 | 392 000 | 10 000 | 9 000 | – | 8 000 | |
| 19 | Structural – Frame | 1 212 000 | 1 285 000 | 33 000 | – | – | 40 000 | |
| 20 | Cladding – GRP | 465 000 | 515 500 | 36 000 | 4 500 | – | 10 000 | |
| 21 | Cladding – Alum | 585 000 | 626 000 | 30 000 | (1 000) | – | 12 000 | |
| 22 | Roof Decking | 370 000 | 381 500 | 15 000 | (13 500) | – | 10 000 | |
| 23 | Windows and Screens | 150 000 | 163 650 | 8 000 | 3 650 | 5 500 | 4 000 | |
| | etc | | | | | | | |
| 41 | Planting | 25 000 | 27 000 | 2 000 | – | – | – | |
| 42 | Fencing | 32 000 | 35 000 | 3 000 | – | – | – | |
| | Sub-total (excluding contract contingencies) | 8 150 000 | 8 430 000 | 245 000 | (102 000) | 10 000 | 132 000 | |
| | Contract Contingencies | 280 000 | 148 000 | – | – | – | – | |
| | TOTALS | 8 430 000 | 8 578 000 | 245 000 | (102 000) | 10 000 | 132 000 | |

❶ Refer projected/final cost record sheet for main parcel attached. Similar sheets prepared for each parcel or where applicable each sub-parcel.

FINANCIAL STATEMENT

CONTRACT:   BLANK REDEVELOPMENT, BLANKSHIRE

for

EMPLOYER   ACME DEVELOPMENTS LTD

REPORT
No: 4 _____            DATE: SEPTEMBER 1987

|   |   | £ | £ | £ |
|---|---|---|---|---|
| 1. | CONTRACT EPC AND MANAGEMENT FEE | | | 8 682 900 |
| | AUTHORIZED EXTRAS/SAVINGS | | | 10 000 |
| | TOTAL AUTHORIZED EPC AND MANAGEMENT FEE | | | 8 692 900 |
| 2. | PROJECTED FINAL COST | 8 578 000 | | |
| 3. | Less   FLUCTUATIONS | 245 000 | 8 333 000 | |
| 4. | Less   OTHER ADJUSTMENTS | 10 000 | | |
| | ADJUSTED EPC (including contingencies) (excluding fluctuations) | 8 323 000 | | |
| 5. | Add   MANAGEMENT FEE (calculated on above Adjusted EPC) | 3% | 249 690 | |
| 6. | PROJECTED FINAL COST AND MANAGEMENT FEE (excluding fluctuations) | | 8 582 690 | 8 582 690 |
| 7. | ESTIMATED OVER/(UNDER) SPEND | | | (110 210) |
| 8. | ALLOWANCE FOR FLUCTUATIONS From Line 3 £   245 000   Add Management Fee ( 3% ) £   7 350 | | | 252 350 |
| 9. | PROJECTED FINAL COST AND MANAGEMENT FEE INCLUDING FLUCTUATIONS | | | 8 835 040 |

Signed ...........................
DEARLE AND HENDERSON
Chartered Quantity Surveyors

**Fig. 4** (Form 1)

## (b) Additional aids and records: forms 6, 7 and 8

Additional forms have been developed for use in the system. These are:

*Form 6 – Accounting record sheet* (Fig. 5). This is used to keep an up-to-date summary of the cost-reimbursable elements of the project.
*Form 7 – Expenditure review form.* This has been developed as an optional form, and its use is shown in Fig. 6. It is helpful for keeping the financial situation under review where individual work-parcel EPCs are being expended in a variety of ways.
*Form 8 – General use materials record* (Fig. 7). This is used to record the value of materials obtained for the scheme, which are for general consumption and are not accounted for by any particular work parcel record sheet. It is a way of making sure that they are picked up in the financial reporting and accounting and do not come as a 'shock' at the end of a project.

### 3.1.3  *The integration of budgetary control and final accounting*

It can be seen that the system has only one source for recording variations and other cost factors on the scheme. In this way there is no need to develop an isolated system for the agreement of the various final accounts for each parcel. The record sheet will eventually have deleted from its title the word 'projected' and will thus be the final cost (final account) for that work-parcel (or, where applicable, subparcel).

It is accepted that different methods of agreeing final accounts are adopted by different parcel contractors. If the agreement of the final account is on the basis of adjusting the original EPC for each variation covered by an instruction, then the record sheet can act as a statement of final account. The example in Fig. 8 shows how the record sheet has been used in this way.

However, in some cases parcel contractors may present their accounts for checking and agreement by the management contractor and quantity surveyor. When agreed the figures can be included in the record sheet in the manner shown in Fig. 9.

However, to achieve the maximum integration from the system it will be necessary for the quantity surveyor to ensure that certain steps are taken.

| ACCOUNTING RECORD SHEET – COST REIMBURSABLE | | | | | | | | JOB NO: 5000 |
|---|---|---|---|---|---|---|---|---|
| CONTRACT: BLANK DEVELOPMENT, BLANKSHIRE FOR ACME DEVELOPMENTS LTD. | | | | | | | | |
| PARCEL REF: SITE MANAGEMENT COSTS | | | | | CONTRACTOR: FAST TRACK (U.K.) LTD. | | | |
| APPLICATION NO: | DATE | LABOUR £ | MATERIALS £ | PLANT £ | TOTAL £ | FLUCTUATIONS INCLUDED IN TOTAL £ | RUNNING TOTALS TOTAL £ | FLUCTUATIONS £ |
| 1 | JUNE '87 | 6858.75 | – | – | 6858.75 | – | 6858.75 | – |
| 2 | JULY '87 | 10460.00 | – | – | 10460.00 | 405.00 | 17318.75 | 405.00 |
| 3 | AUG '87 | 11218.00 | – | – | 11218.00 | 1307.27 | 28536.75 | 1712.27 |
| 4 | SEPT '87 | (P)13000.00 | – | – | (P)13000.00 | (P)2000.00 | (P)41536.75 | (P)3712.27 |
| TOTALS | | | | | | | | |

* (P) PROVISIONAL

Fig. 5 (Form 6)

| EXPENDITURE REVIEW: | | | | JOB NO: 5000 |
|---|---|---|---|---|

| CONTRACT *BLANK REDEVELOPMENT* FOR *ACME DEVELOPMENTS LTD.* | PARCEL REF: *EXCAVATION AND FILLING* |
|---|---|

| SECTION | PROGRESS   APPLICATION NO: 4 |
|---|---|
| | DATE: *SEPT '87* |

| | LABOUR £ | MATERIALS £ | PLANT £ | TOTAL £ |
|---|---|---|---|---|
| A.   COST REIMBURSABLE | | | | |
| B/Fwd. From Previous Applications | 217.00 | 405.25 | 250.00 | 872.25 |
| This application: | | | | |
| (i) *FAST TRACK (U.K.) LTD.* | 150.00 | 50.00 | — | 200.00 |
| (ii) *GROUNDWORKS LTD* | 350.00 | 40.00 | 300.00 | 690.00 |
| B.   GENERAL USE MATERIALS (Value allocated) | *SAY* | 2000.00 | | 2000.00 |
| C.   FIXED PRICE CONTRACTS | | | | |
| (i) *GROUND WORKS LTD.* | | | | 92700.00 |
| (ii)      — | | | | |
| | TOTAL EXPENDITURE COMMITTED | | | 96 462.25 |
| | LATEST PROJECTED/FINAL COST | | | 108 500 |
| | BALANCE AVAILABLE FOR REMAINDER OF WORK | | | 12037.75 |

FINANCIAL REPORT NO: 4

*THIS PARCEL ALMOST COMPLETE. FIXED PRICE CONTRACT INCLUDES CONTINGENCIES — CAN COST NEXT FINANCIAL REPORT*

*Note* This form can be used for different parcels at different times on a project to assist the surveyor in forming an overall view of the parcel budget and current committed expenditure.

**Fig. 6 (Form 7)**

| CONTRACT: **BLANK REDEVELOPMENT FOR ACME REDEVELOPMENTS LTD.** | | | JOB NO: 5000 |
|---|---|---|---|
| SUMMARY OF GENERAL USE MATERIALS | | | |
| APPLICATION NR: | DATE | VALUE £ | RUNNING TOTAL £ |
| 1 | JUNE '87 | 1307.30 | — |
| 2 | JULY '87 | 2703.75 | 4011.05 |
| 3 | AUG '87 | (P) 1500.00 | (P) 5511.05 |
| 4 | SEPT '87 | (P) 2500.00 | (P) 8011.05 |

*Note* The value of materials can be added to the projected/final cost system under an appropriate heading together with other summary matters.

**Fig. 7** (Form 8)

PROJECTED/FINAL COST RECORD SHEET

CONTRACT  BLANK REDEVELOPMENT BLANKSHIRE

WORK PARCEL REF  23 WINDOWS AND SCREENS

JOB NO:  5000

SUB PARCEL REF  ACE WINDOWS LTD.

1. CONTRACT EPC

   A. Cost reimbursable allocation

   B. Fixed-price allocation

| | | | A £ | B £ |
|---|---|---|---|---|
| | | | — | 150 000.00 |

2. ESTIMATED VALUE OF A/SO INSTRUCTIONS

| A/SO/1 No | | Classification | | | | A £ | B £ |
|---|---|---|---|---|---|---|---|
| | | Non-EPC £ | B £ | Adj £ | EPC £ | | |
| 29 | PLACE SUB-CONTRACT | — | — | — | — | — | 2150.00 |
| 36 | AMEND GLASS-NORTH WING | — | — | — | — | — | 4600.00 |
| 43 | OMIT W/W LOCKS w/w 57.99 | — | — | — | — | — | (3750.00) |
| 50 | EMERGENCY WK. (LATE ORDER) | — | 175.00 | — | — | — | 2195.75 |
| 55 | ADDITIONAL W/W5 WEST WING | — | — | — | — | — | 723.29 |
| 64 | UPVC SUBSILL W/W 31.36 | — | — | — | — | — | (124.50) |
| 81 | AMEND GLAZING BEAD W/W7 | | | | | | |
| | | | | | | | |
| | | | | | | | |
| | | | | | | | |
| | | | | | | | |
| | | | | | | | |
| | | | | | | | |
| | | | | | | | |
| | C/Fwd | — | 1715.00 | — | 5794.54 | — | 150 000.00 |

2. CON'T

| A/SO/1 No: | | Classifications | | | | A £ |
|---|---|---|---|---|---|---|
| | | Non-EPC £ | B £ | Adj £ | EPC £ | |
| | B/FWD | — | 1715.00 | — | 5794.54 | 50 000.00 |
| | | | | | | |
| | | | | | | |
| | | | | | | |
| | | | | | | |
| | ADJUSTED EPC | — | ///// | | 5794.54 | 5794.54 |

| | | | | | | A £ |
|---|---|---|---|---|---|---|
| | ADJUSTED EPC | — | 1715.00 | ///// | | 1715.00 |
| | | | | | | 155 794.54 |

3. OTHER ADJUSTMENTS

| | A £ | B £ |
|---|---|---|
| | | |

157 509.54

4. FLUCTUATIONS

INCLUDED IN 1-3 ABOVE = £6950.00

5. CONTINGENCY

| | A £ |
|---|---|
| | — |
| | 157 509.54 |

PROJECTED/FINAL COST  — 157 509.54

① Figures included in these columns are net extra or omission.

② This sum also includes the parcel contractor's loss and expense caused by the management contractor's delay in placing order. All agreed loss and expense for sub-parcel placed against appropriate AI or if generally applicable loss and expense can be included in items other adjustments.

③ This represents final assessment/calculation of fluctuations in parcel.

④ This figure transferred to a separate sheet which contains the Q.S. parcel contractor's and management contractor's agreement to figure by signatures.

Fig. 8 (Form 3)

(PRIME COST RECORD SHEET)

CONTRACT **BLANK REDEVELOPMENT**

WORK PARCEL REF **23 - WINDOWS AND SCREENS**   JOB No.: **5000**

SUB PARCEL REF **ACE WINDOWS LTD.**

| | A £ | B £ |
|---|---|---|
| | | 150 000.00 |

1. CONTRACT EPC

   A. Cost reimbursable allocation

   B. Fixed-price allocation

2. ESTIMATED VALUE OF A/SO INSTRUCTIONS

| A/SO/1 No | Classification | | | |
|---|---|---|---|---|
| | Non-EPC A £ | B £ | Adj EPC A £ | B £ |
| 29 PLACE SUB-CONTRACT | Refer below | - | - | - |
| 36 AMEND GLASS-NORTH WING | DITTO | - | - | - |
| 43 OMIT W/W LOCKS N/W 57.99 | DITTO | - | - | - |
| 50 EMERGENCY WK (LATE ORDER) | DITTO | - | - | - |
| 55 ADDITIONAL W/WS WESTWING | DITTO | - | - | - |
| 64 UPVC SUB-SILL W/W 31.36 | DITTO | - | - | - |
| 81 AMEND GLAZING BEAD W/W7 | DITTO | - | - | - |
| ❶ AGREED ADJUSTMENT OF SUB-CONTRACTOR'S WORKS AS ATTACHED FINAL ACCOUNT | - | 1715.00 | - | 5794.54 |
| | | | | |
| | | | | |
| ❸ | | | | |
| C/Fwd | - | 1715.00 | - | 5794.54 |

| | A £ | B £ |
|---|---|---|
| | | 150 000.00 |
| | - | 150 000.00 |

❶ Figures included in these columns are net extras or omissions.

❷ This represents final assessment/calculation of fluctuations in parcel.

❸ If parcel contractor's final account not suitably endorsed this figure transferred to a separate sheet which contains the Q.S. parcel contractor's and management contractor's agreement to figure by signature.

---

2. CON'T

| A/SO/1 No: | Classification | | | | | | A £ | B £ |
|---|---|---|---|---|---|---|---|---|
| | Non-EPC A £ | B £ | Adj EPC A £ | B £ | | | | |
| B/FWD | - | 1715.00 | - | 5794.54 | | | | 150 000.00 |
| | | | | | | | | |
| ADJUSTED EPC | ///// | ///// | - | 5794.54 | | | - | 5794.54 |
| | - | 1715.00 | ///// | ///// | | | - | 155794.54 |
| | | | | | | | - | 1715.00 |
| | | | | | | | - | 157509.54 |

3. OTHER ADJUSTMENTS    A £    B £

4. FLUCTUATIONS
   INCLUDED IN 1-3 ABOVE = £6960.00 ❷
   (REFER ATTACHED DEFECTS
   /FINAL ACCOUNT )

5. CONTINGENCY

PROJECTED/FINAL COST

| | A £ | B £ |
|---|---|---|
| | - | 157509. |
| | | 15750 |

Fig. 9 (Form 3)

(1) When a work-parcel contract tender is received a reconciliation statement (form 5), an example of which is shown in Fig. 1, will need to be prepared. This reconciliation statement presents the cost information contained in the work-parcel tender in a slightly different manner than is normally found.

(2) The quantity surveyor must insist upon a well-disciplined system of issuing instructions, especially for those that vary the contract. In the examples shown every instruction is confirmed by an architect's or supervising officer's instruction, and these are used as a basis for control.

(3) When using a management contract there should be no need to include provisional sums in any work-parcel tender document. However, in some cases it may be appropriate to show a tenderer that an amount will be required for the cost of some undefined work. Note that on the reconciliation statement space is provided for provisional sums to be listed. This can be used as a check that the architect or supervising officer has resolved each provisional sum. Provisional sums are adjusted as early as possible, in order to avoid the possibility of double accounting.

### 3.1.4 *Contingencies*

Contingencies are sometimes included in the work parcel as well as in the balance of the scheme. The reason for including a contingency in a parcel contract is to provide a parcel contractor with an indication of the team's estimated contingency for the parcel. In this way the parcel contractor's expectation for additional costs can be limited. Alternatively, all contingencies can be maintained outside the parcel contracts in the form of a contract contingency or an employer-maintained contingency.

### 3.1.5 *Valuations for payment*

Some people have described a management contractor as a banker for the employer under this arrangement. He will make payments to all who are engaged in the construction project (except independently appointed consultants or directly employed contractors) upon receipt of the employer's instructions. These instructions can be issued in a

```
                    QUANTITY SURVEYORS REPORT  SHEET 1

                    VALUATION No. 4  for SEPTEMBER 1987
```

Works            BLANK REDEVELOPMENT
                 PARK LANE
                 BLANKSHIRE

Employer         ACME DEVELOPMENTS LTD
                 HIGH FIELD HOUSE
                 EAST STREET
                 WEST BLANKSHIRE

Architect/       DESIGN & DESIGN
Supervising      ARCHITECTS
Officer          CONSERVATIONS ROW
                 BLANKSHIRE

Management       FAST TRACK (UK) LTD
Contractor       PLENTY DRIVE
                 BANK-UPON-THAMES

|  | Contract Value £ | Fluctuations £ | Total £ |
|---|---|---|---|
| Management Contractors Work | 105 000 | 1 505 | 106 505 |
| Parcel Contractors Work | 842 000 | 13 060 | 855 060 |
| Sub-Total | 947 000 | 14 565 | 961 565 |
| Management Fee  3  % on £ 961 565 | | | 28 847 |
| Total Carried Forward | | | 990 412 |

**Fig. 10** (Form 9, sheet 1)

CONTRACT: BLANK REDEVELOPMENT

     for

   ACME DEVELOPMENTS LTD

QUANTITY SURVEYORS
REPORT SHEET 2

Valuation No.  4   for   September 1987         £

| | | £ |
|---|---|---|
| Total brought forward | | 990 412 |
| Less Retention | | |
| Parcel Contractors  5  % on £ 855 060 | 42 753 | |
| Management Fee  10  % on £ 28 847 | 2 885 | |
| | 45 638 | |

Deduct   release of rentention on issue
of certificates of practical completion
and/or making good defects

| | | | |
|---|---|---|---|
| Parcel Contractors<br>Management Fee | – | – | 45 638 |
| TOTAL DUE TO DATE | | | 944 774 |
| Less Amount Previously Certified | | | 685 070 |
| BALANCE RECOMMENDED FOR PAYMENT | | £ | 259 704 |

*Dearle & Henderson*  DEARLE AND HENDERSON
                          Chartered Quantity Surveyors

**Fig. 10** (Form 9, sheet 2)

variety of ways, the most common being through the quantity surveyor's report. This report is normally supported by a formal certificate of payment from the appropriate consultant.

The quantity surveyor's report resembles a conventional contract valuation, and most management contracts require that the employer will honour such payments within a set period from receipt of an architect's or supervising officer's certificate of payment.

A standard form 9 of a quantity surveyor's report has been developed for use in the system, and a completed typical copy is shown in Fig. 10.

Supporting this form will be a copy of a report/valuation build-up which will show the value of payments to each parcel contractor or directly employed resource. Depending on the exact wording of the form of parcel contract adopted for the project, it is not usual for the architect or quantity surveyor to be required to ascertain whether payments have been discharged by the management contractor. However, where some form of design warranty or agreement exists between the employer and the parcel contractor, a condition of that agreement might mean that the employer will discharge payment directly if the management contractor defaults.

Reference was made in Part One to the subject of retention. In the form of management contract contained in Appendix A provision is made for the employer to retain a percentage of the management fee. It is also usual for the employer to retain a percentage of the value of the parcel contractor's payments, but this is arranged by agreement with the management contractor. In cases where the employer does not retain a percentage of the value of parcel contracts, the management contractor will usually retain such a percentage by virtue of the terms of the contract with the parcel contractor.

When the final costs of the project have been established the *final* quantity surveyor's report will be endorsed by the management contractor to show that in the management contractor's opinion no further payments are due under the contract.


### 3.1.6 *Settlement of work-parcel accounts*

The procedures for settling the final accounts of work-parcel contractors under a management contract resemble those used for the settlement of nominated subcontract accounts under conventional contracts. However, the following should be noted.

(1) Agreement to the work-parcel account is between the management contractor and the work-parcel contractor. The consultant quantity surveyor will endorse the agreed statement of final account as being prepared in accordance with the terms of the management contract.
(2) The consultant quantity surveyor will check that when an account is prepared by a work-parcel contractor it does not contain any costs that the employer is not required to pay under the contract.
(3) Where the projected/final cost record sheet is used as a financial statement in the manner shown in the earlier example, it is advisable to obtain an endorsement to this form from the work-parcel contractor, management contractor and consultant quantity surveyor.

### 3.1.7 *Adjustment of the EPC*

The management contract will define the items that comprise the EPC. In the case of the form of management contract provided in this manual the definition is included as an appendix to the contract. The contract will also describe the basis upon which the EPC will be finally adjusted. This basis is most important, since the finally adjusted EPC is usually the figure on which most fees are calculated, in particular the fee of the management contractor.

In management contracts based on the philosophy of the low-risk professional agreement, the reasons for allowing an adjustment of the EPC are wide and generally only seek to exclude increases in the value of the works that have been caused by the management contractor's negligence or poor performance in the more critical elements of his service. However, management contracts can include more-restrictive clauses.

When the management fee is a lump sum the contract will usually include a provision that no adjustment to the fee will be made unless the finally adjusted EPC differs from the contract EPC by a prescribed factor (for example ±10%). However, in all management contracts reasonableness should prevail in the matter of adjusting the EPC. It must be remembered that many contract EPCs are formulated while the scheme is at an early stage of design, and it would be unreasonable to insist upon severely restrictive EPC adjustment clauses.

In practice, if the EPC clauses are sufficiently wide in their construction a common-sense attitude will be developed by all parties. However, for each increase or decrease in the value of the works it must be assessed whether it should form part of the final adjusted EPC. It should be borne in mind that a 'swings and roundabouts' situation generally exists in management contracting.

This aspect is well illustrated by the case of increases that occur in the value of works due entirely to a difference from the estimated price and an actual price achieved in competitive tendering (after making all other adjustments such as inflation). In such cases quantity surveyors are often tempted to suggest that the increased value in these circumstances should not form part of the finally adjusted EPC. The reason offered is that the management contractor's responsibility is to contain costs within the contract EPC, and the extra has occurred because the estimate was initially pitched at too low a level.

This attitude is unsound for two reasons. First, the contract EPC is a budget to which all parties to the contract are committed, and the opportunity should have been taken by the consultant quantity surveyor in particular and by others in general to assess whether the EPC was realistic and achievable. Thus, any underestimation by the management contractor is almost equally shared by others. Secondly, with competitive tenders being sought for more than 50 parcel contracts accepted tenders are generally a mixture of increases to and decreases from the original EPC.

Hence, if increases are ruled out of the adjusted EPC, so too should decreases. Of course, it might be in the employer's overall interest to include such adjustments when the decreases are greater than the increases.

### 3.1.8 *Depreciation/write-off values for purchased plant, etc.*

It was stated at the commencement of this manual that because management contracting employs many of the quantity surveyor's conventional techniques it would be impossible to highlight every aspect involved in the fulfilment of the quantity surveyor's role. However, it is worth noting that the management contract will involve the quantity surveyor in many aspects of cost-reimbursable accounting, especially where the preliminary work parcels form part of the EPC.

One aspect that must be determined early is the method for

calculating the depreciation of purchased plant and equipment. Although many large items will be obtained under hiring agreements, others will have a capital value. In the case of newly purchased items depreciation can be calculated using conventional writing-down allowances. In cases of items which are not new a formula will have to be agreed for assessing the capital value. The contract period for most management contracts is much less than the capital life of plant and equipment. Hence, agreement will have to be made within the depreciation calculation for residual values and a credit obtained for this residual value from the management contractor at the end of the contract.

The quantity surveyor will also have to ensure that realistic checking procedures are established for small items of expenditure. Many sites under management contracts maintain a petty cash system for emergency purchases, such as site stationery, and these (if not forming part of the management fee) must be monitored accurately. However, the quantity surveyor will not be able to exercise lengthy verification procedures on relatively small items of expenditure. In such cases it will be sufficient for the quantity surveyor to establish a limit of expenditure for the contract for petty cash payments above which prior approval must be sought from the quantity surveyor.

### 3.1.9  Loss and expense

The validation and evaluation of loss and expense on management contracts follow conventional rules. However, the pattern of loss and expense settlements on management contracts are different from those found under conventional contracts.

The quantity surveyor will probably be involved in settling a large number of relatively small amounts which should in all cases have been first examined and evaluated by the management contractor. The management contractor will, of course, attempt to eradicate the causes of loss and expense by efficiently managing the works. However, genuine cases arise where one parcel contractor is disrupted or delayed because of the acts or omissions of another, or in some cases by the management contractor. Where it can be clearly shown that one parcel contractor has caused disruption to others the management contractor must use a system of contra-charging to ensure that the employer does not bear the resultant costs.

In other cases, however, the employer will be at risk for loss and expense incurred, especially that resulting from factors qualifying under the contract as grounds for extension of the contract period. The quantity surveyor must monitor potential causes of delays and disruption which might give rise to loss and expense, and ensure that the management contractor is in a position to allocate responsibility for loss and expense.

## 3.2  Cost and productivity monitoring

The success of the budgetary control system described above will be dependent on the quality of data made available to the quantity surveyor. Conventional tendering and contractual arrangements are designed to resolve the issues having a major impact on cost before the employer becomes committed to a contract. How successfully this is achieved is outside the scope of this manual.

However, management contracts are commonly employed on schemes which have not been fully designed when construction is required to commence. Hence, the issues having an impact on cost – and more importantly the ability to forecast cost accurately – are variable. The lack of design completion may have arisen for a variety of reasons, but the two main reasons are the following.

(1) An accelerated programme which precludes much of the time normally required to develop the design in advance of construction found under conventional contracts.
(2) The complexity or uncertainty of the scheme means that even with a relatively generous programme not all design solutions are possible, and construction is needed to test the buildability of the ultimate design. This is very much more applicable to refurbishment schemes.

To assist in budgetary control there exists under many management contracts a need to test the economic viability of the proposed design solutions. The quantity surveyor will be expected to interpret cost and productivity data in a manner that can be reported to the employer who will then be able to make the proper choices and decisions.

It is accepted that quantity surveyors are not extensively trained in the techniques of operational site management and work study, but they have the ability to analyse data and use this as a basis for making financial projections. For schemes that require a special emphasis on cost and productivity monitoring the management contractor should be asked to include appropriate facilities in his arrangements. To this end the design team will need to state clearly the objectives to be achieved by the monitoring arrangements. These objectives will be shaped by several factors, of which the principal ones are repetition, site-management resources and cost reimbursement.

### 3.2.1  *Repetition*

Many schemes have economies to be obtained through repetition in both physical work and management/organization. In some cases repetition is present due to a large number of units making up a total project (for example, housing). In other cases repetition is a product of scale. Although judgement by the professional team and the pressure of competition will force a view to be taken on the economies achievable through repetition, very few positive attempts are made in construction contracts to penetrate this aspect.

Management contracts provide an opportunity to investigate such economies in detail. In some cases employers might be persuaded to approve expenditure on a pilot study to test feasibility before undertaking major construction expenditure. This is particularly relevant to multi-unit schemes (for example housing, system-building programmes) and refurbishment.

### 3.2.2  *Site-management resources*

Site-management and facilities costs typically fall in the range 10–20% of total costs. This represents a substantial proportion of the cost of a scheme and where reimbursed on a cost basis costs, will need to be controlled effectively to remain within budgets.

In such circumstances it is essential that investigation into methods of site organization and management be built into the arrangements in order to obtain the most efficient use from the resources employed. This investigation can also assess methods of site (pre-)fabrication through the examination of the provision of site-based workshops.

### 3.2.3 *Cost-reimbursement aspects*

With a proportion of the costs of any management contract settled on a cost-reimbursement basis, it is essential that the quantity surveyor's forecasts take into account the impact on real costs of the contractor's operations. Work-study techniques are able to measure productivity and the effects of the 'learning curve' inherent in any new construction project.

Visual aids such as histograms assist the quantity surveyor's presentation of overall cost forecast. Relatively complex calculations can be presented in a digestible pictorial format.

## 3.3 Financial projections and studies

It is acknowledged in this manual that each employer will place slightly different demands on the quantity surveyor for financial management services, and for that matter on the professional team generally. Several commentators have proffered the view that the quantity surveyor's role in providing financial services is expanding. Apart from the more specialized areas of financial advice which are not required for every scheme (most notably in the areas of taxation and grants), some services are becoming a regular feature. It must be appreciated that in a manual devoted to procurement aspects of management contracting it is only possible to illustrate how quantity surveyors' financial services relate to the arrangement.

### 3.3.1 *Cash-flow projections*

It is a common requirement for quantity surveyors to provide projections of the monthly cash flow. Many employers need to make arrangements to ensure finance is available to meet the commitments of their various projects, so realistic cash-flow projections are essential. Standard approaches and a computer program have been developed to produce the more customary cash-flow calculations.

These are based on the conventional expenditure curve known as the 'lazy S'. Management contracts often distort this expenditure curve, and the monthly expenditure pattern can take the form of a straight incline rather than a gradual curve. The management contractor's programme will assist in the estimation of monthly expenditure, and quantity surveyors should take special note of the effects of accelerated expenditure patterns on fluctuations and inflation forecasts.

### 3.3.2 *Risk analysis*

Risk analysis has been more comprehensively employed in long-term strategic programmes and projects. However, its application to projects of lesser expenditure has been successful. It is not only concerned with major risks, but is also used to assess the effects of the common occurrences that affect all construction projects.

Management contracts often involve the employer taking greater risk for costs than under conventional contracts. For example, most of the costs associated with bad weather and strikes will tend to fall on the employer. For contracts that extend over several years the range of out-turn costs can vary to an extent where the employer needs a view taken on the probability of financial targets being achieved.

Although the budgetary control system described in this manual alerts the employer to the amount of finance for which provision should be made at any given time, most employers require a view on the chances of that figure being amended. Risk-analysis techniques can be employed to:

(1) Identify the risks associated with the project in a way that reflects their particular impact on the scheme;
(2) Assess the effects of these risks which the quantity surveyor can present in terms of cost prediction;
(3) Promote action to be taken to mitigate the effects of risks, this being commonly termed 'risk management'.

### 3.3.3 *Value management*

Over the years quantity surveyors have developed a range of techniques and services which for convenience can be grouped under the title *value management*.

These include life cycle costing, value engineering, energy and maintenance cost audit and similar techniques which are devoted to evaluating the economic performance of buildings or certain components.

Management contracts contain the potential for the quantity surveyor to obtain more detailed cost information than is normally available under conventional arrangements. This should have a beneficial impact on the quantity surveyor's ability to provide value management services.

*Part Four*

---

# APPENDICES:
# CONTRACTS, FORMS
# AND DOCUMENTS

---

# *Appendix A*

---

# Framework for a management contract agreement

---

*Notes*

This framework has been presented as follows:

(1) Principal headings are shown in **boldface** type;
(2) Typical clauses follow in normal type;
(3) Although typical clauses cover the major aspects of low-risk management contracts, they would need to be amended or supplemented as necessary to cover any specific requirement of a particular contract.

AGREEMENT made the — day of 198 between the Employer, as set out in the Schedule hereto (hereinafter called 'The Employer') of the one part and named in the Schedule hereto (hereinafter called 'the Contractor') of the other part.

WHEREAS:

*Typical clauses*

(1) The Employer requires.................................................................................
hereinafter called 'the Works'.
(2) The Employer has appointed.....................................................................
......................................................... as set out in the Schedule hereto
(hereinafter called 'the Supervising Officer') to design and prepare a
specification and drawings for the purpose.
(3) The Employer has appointed.....................................................................
......................................................... as set out in the Schedule hereto
(hereinafter called the 'the Quantity Surveyor') to prepare estimates, tender
documents, and monitor cost.
(4) The Quantity Surveyor has prepared a document setting out a description
of the work (hereinafter called the 'Tender Document') which, together with
the drawings listed therein and specification form the basis of tender.
(5) The Contractor has submitted an Estimate of Prime Cost of the Works
based on the Tender Document at current prices and rates of wages as set
out in the Schedule hereto (hereinafter called 'The Estimate of Prime Cost')
and agreed it with the Quantity Surveyor.
(6) The Contractor has agreed to undertake the Works in accordance with the
Tender Document upon the terms and subject to the conditions hereinafter
prescribed.

## 1. Architect/supervising officer

## Now it is hereby agreed:

## The Architect/Supervising Officer will:

*Typical clauses*

(1) Prepare such drawings and specifications and furnish such instructions
from time to time as may be necessary for the execution of the Works.
(2) Provide supervision necessary for the implementation of the design.
(3) Give in writing any instruction arising from the testing of the validity of the
design or for variations or any other matter affecting the Works.
(4) Monitor and authorize changes in the Time and Progress Schedule as
defined in Clause 4.
(5) Give a Certificate of Practical Completion when in his reasonable opinion
this has been achieved.

(6) Issue a Schedule of Defects as defined in Clause 7.

N.B. The above duties to be amended where necessary by reference to the employer's tender documents and/or contractor's submission.

## 2. Quantity surveyor

### The Quantity Surveyor will:

*Typical clauses*

(1) In conjunction with the Contractor provide Bills of Quantities or such other Tendering Documents as thought fit for despatch to the sub-works* contractors and suppliers.
(2) Audit expenditure by the Contractor on items included in the Prime Cost as defined in Appendix 'A' hereof.
(3) Make periodic reports as set out in Clause 11 hereof.
(4) Adjust the Estimate of Prime Cost as work proceeds to make allowance for any of the following.
    (a) Actual expenditure on items for which Provisional Sums were allowed.
    (b) Any instructions or variation given by the Architect/Supervising Officer.
    (c) Any change in Government legislation, Government direction or in market conditions.
    (d) Changes in Time and Progress Schedule as authorized by the Architect/Supervising Officer.
    (e) Extension of time (under Clause 4 hereof).
    (f) Any increase or decrease in expenditure by the Contractor on any item within the definition of Prime Cost caused by decrease or unavoidable increase in the rates and prices used in the Estimate of Prime Cost.
    (g) Unavoidable changes in conditions under which the work is carried out and any other circumstances in which in the opinion of the Architect/Supervising Officer would be fair and reasonable for the Estimate of Prime Cost to be increased or decreased.

The estimate when finally adjusted shall be referred to as the 'Final Adjusted Estimate of Prime Cost'.

N.B. The above duties to be amended where necessary by reference to the employer's tender documents and/or contractor's submission.

## 3. The Contractor

### The Contractor will:

*Typical clauses*

(1) Organize the execution of the Works including putting forward methods for carrying out the Works for discussion beforehand with the Architect/

* Delete where applicable.

Supervising Officer and the Quantity Surveyor and after such discussion the Contractor, having taken into account such comments of the Architect/Supervising Officer and Quantity Surveyor as he thinks fit, will assume responsibility for the execution of the Works in accordance with the drawings and the specifications supplied and instructions furnished to him from time to time.

(2) Implement the Works in an economical manner consistent with the sound workmanship and within the agreed Time and Progress Schedule.

(3) Provide competent supervision for the Works, engage labour, order and check all materials and generally perform everything necessary for the proper execution of the Works.

(4) Provide surveying staff to monitor the cost of individual activities as required by and in conjunction with the Quantity Surveyor.

(5) Keep proper books in accordance with the Contractor's costing system for management contracts which will be open at all reasonable times for the inspection of the Quantity Surveyor or other representatives of the Employer and provide copies of such documents as the Quantity Surveyor may from time to time require.

N.B. The above duties to be amended where necessary by reference to the employer's tender documents and/or contractor's submission.

## 4. Time and Progress Schedule

*Typical clauses*

As soon as possible after appointment and receipt of the necessary drawings specifications and instructions from the Architect/Supervising Officer and the events in Clause 3(1) hereof have taken place and before work starts on site, the Contractor will put forward a Time and Progress Schedule for the Works showing the various stages and dates of Practical Completion. On acceptance by the Architect/Supervising Officer this will become the Contract Time and Progress Schedule. If in the reasonable opinion of the Architect/Supervising Officer the Works thereafter are delayed

(a) by reason of any instruction or variation given by the Architect/Supervising Officer pursuant to Clause 1(1)(2) and (3) except instructions relating to defects as Clause 7;

(b) by reason of the Contractor not having received in due time necessary instructions drawings or specification from the Architect/Supervising Officer whereby the progress of the Works is materially affected;

(c) by any material interference by the Employer in the carrying out of the Works;

(d) by any other cause beyond the control of the Contractor.

Then the Architect/Supervising Officer shall allow a fair and reasonable extension of time.

## 5. Damages for non-completion

*Typical clause*

If the Contractor fails to complete the Works by or within the times fixed under Clause 4 hereof, and the Architect/Supervising Officer certifies in writing that the same ought reasonably to have been completed, the Contractor shall pay or allow to the Employer a sum calculated at the rate per week shown in the Schedule as liquidated and ascertained damages for the period during which the said work shall so remain or have remained incomplete.

## 6. Notices, Fees and statutory obligations

*Typical clause*

The Contractor shall comply with any Act of Parliament and any instrument rule or order made under an Act of Parliament or any regulation or Bye-Law of any Local Authority or of any statutory undertaking which has jurisdiction with regard to the work insofar as such Acts of Parliament, instruments, rules, orders, regulations and Bye-Laws shall apply to the Contractor in carrying out the work. The Contractor before making any variations necessitated by such compliance shall give written notice to the Architect/Supervising Officer specifying and giving the reason for such variation and, unless the Architect/Supervising Officer shall object, shall proceed with the work after the expiry of seven days therefrom. The variation necessitated shall be deemed to be a variation of the work.

## 7. Defects arising from these Works

*Typical clause*

Any work, materials or goods which are not in accordance with the contract and for which the Architect/Supervising Officer has issued instructions for removal from site pursuant to Clause 1(2) and (3) or any defects, shrinkage or other faults that arise in the Works either during the course of the Works or within six months of practical completion, or in the case of service installations twelve months, except defects attributed to faults in design or to the occupation of the Works by the Employer or its tenants, shall be made good by the Contractor at his own expense. The Architect/Supervising Officer shall certify the date when in his opinion the Contractor's obligations under this Clause have been discharged.

## 8. Unfixed materials

*Typical clause*

All unfixed materials intended for the Works shall become the property of the Employer after the  Contractor has received payment on any certificate which includes their value but, subject to Clause 16, the Contractor shall be liable for any damage to or loss of such materials whilst in his custody or under his control.

## 9. Excess materials

*Typical clause*

If, at any time during or on the conclusion of the Works and upon measurement by the Quantity Surveyor, the materials brought on the site for which the Contractor has received payment are found to exceed substantially the amount required according to the drawings specification Bills of Quantities or remeasurement the excess is to be credited by the Contractor to the Employer at invoice value, and any excess material remaining on the site shall be removed by the Contractor at his own expense.

## 10. Sub-/works* contractors and suppliers

*Typical clauses*

(1) Sub-/works* contractors and suppliers will be appointed by the Contractor in agreement with the Architect/Supervising Officer and in time for the Contractor to comply with the Time and Progress Schedules. Prices for all sub-/works* contracts and supplies shall be submitted to the Quantity Surveyor before such sub-/works* contracts are placed.

(2) Competitive prices will be sought for all sub-/works* contracts and supplies unless in the opinion of the Architect/Supervising Officer, after consultation with the Quantity Surveyor, it would be advantageous to appoint a particular sub-/works* contractor or supplier.

(3) The Contractor shall not be obliged to appoint any sub-/works* contractor or supplier who will not enter into a sub-/works* contract acceptable to the Contractor in accordance with his conditions for sub-/works* contracts and in such cases as the Architect/Supervising Officer or the Contractor shall consider appropriate execute with the Employer a form of warranty in a form approved by the Contractor in consultation with the Architect/Supervising Officer which warrants the sufficiency and suitability of the design of the relevant sub-/works* contract work, including the selection of materials.

## 11. Quantity Surveyor's report

*Typical clause*

The Quantity Surveyor will each month draw up a report showing the expenditure by the Contractor during the previous month on items of Prime Cost

* Delete where applicable.

as defined in Appendix (a) hereof and will include therein the proportion of the management fee less 10% as defined in Appendix 'B' hereof accrued to date and calculated in proportion to the value of the Adjusted Estimate of Prime Cost committed to date.

## 12. Architect's/Supervising Officer's Certificate

*Typical clause*

Within seven days of receiving the Quantity Surveyor's report the Architect/ Supervising Officer shall issue a Certificate showing the amount of the Prime Cost and Proportion of the management fee as reported by the Quantity Surveyor, less the amount already certified.

## 13. Supervising Officer's Final Certificate

*Typical clause*

Upon the expiration of a period of six months from Practical Completion, twelve months for services installations, or when the Architect/Supervising Officer issues a certificate of making good defects under Clause 7, whichever is the later the Architect/Supervising Officer shall issue a Final Certificate showing the full amount of the Prime Cost as reported by the Quantity Surveyor and the full amount of the management fee based on the Final Adjusted Estimate of Prime Cost less the amounts already certified.

## 14. Payments

*Typical clause*

The Employer will pay to the Contractor the amount stated in the Supervising Officer's certificates within fourteen (14) days of the date of issue.

## 14A. Fair wages

*Typical clause*

The Contractor shall in respect of all persons employed by him (whether in the execution of this Agreement or otherwise) in every factory, workshop or place occupied or used by him for the execution of this Agreement comply with the Conditions of the Fair Wages Resolution passed by the House of Commons on the 14th October 1946 or any amendment thereof.

## 15. Injury to persons and property

*Typical clauses*

(1) The Contractor shall be liable for, and shall indemnify the Employer against any expense, liability, loss, claim or proceeding whatsoever arising under any Statute or in Common Law in respect of personal injury to, or the death of, any person whomsoever arising out of, or in the course of, or caused in the carrying out of, the Works unless due to any act or neglect of the Employer, or any person for whom the Employer is responsible.

(2) Except for such loss or damage as is at the risk of the Employer under Clause 16 hereof, the Contractor shall be liable for, and shall indemnify the Employer against any expense, liability, loss, claim or proceedings in respect of any injury or damage whatsoever to any property, real or personal, insofar as such injury or damage arising out of, or in the course of, or by reason of the carrying out of the Works, provided always that the same is due to any negligence, omission or the default of the Contractor, his servants or agents, or of any sub-/works* contractor, or his servants or agents.

(3) Without prejudice to the liability to indemnify the Employer contained in this Clause the Contractor shall maintain insurance and cause any sub-/works* contractors to maintain insurance necessary to cover the liability of the Contractor and any sub-/works* contractor against the risk specified in sub-Clauses (1) and (2) of this Clause and produce the receipts for insurance premiums when requested.

## 16. Damage to Works

*Typical clauses*

(1) All work executed and all unfixed materials and goods intended for, delivered to, and placed on or immediately adjacent to the Works in respect of which work under this Agreement is being effected, but excluding any unfixed materials and goods temporarily placed in a separate compound, shall be at the sole risk of the Employer† as regards loss or damage by fire, storm, tempest, lightning, explosion, flood bursting or overflowing of water tanks apparatus or pipes, earthquake, aircraft or anything dropped therefrom, aerial objects riot and civil commotion.

(2) Residual risk in respect of the Works and all unfixed materials and goods intended for the Works, and all normal insurable risk of loss or damage in respect of temporary works, temporary buildings, plant, tools and equipment and those materials placed in any separate compound shall be insured by the Contractor.

* Delete where applicable.
† Alternative to be used where risk to be borne by the Contractor.

## 17.  Determination by Employer

*Typical clauses*

(1) The Employer may determine the Contractor's employment under this Agreement at any time by giving written notice to the Contractor but without prejudice to the rights of the parties accrued to the date of determination and to the operation of the following provisions of this Clause.

(2) In such event the Employer shall
   (a) pay the Contractor the Prime Cost of the work as contained in the Quantity Surveyor's report prepared as soon as possible after the notice of determination. Such reports to include such further expenditure as the Quantity Surveyor may certify as being unavoidably incurred or incurred at the request of the Employer;
   (b) pay the Contractor a management fee based on the Quantity Surveyor's estimated value as stated in the Quantity Surveyor's report in (a) above;
   (c) indemnify the Contractor against any claims made in respect of all subcontractors and others in relation to the Works and arising from such determination.

Provided that the Contractor shall in any subcontract made by him in connection with and for the purpose of this Agreement take power to determine such subcontract and shall exercise such power forthwith upon the Employer exercising the power under the terms of this Clause.

## 17A.  Determination by Employer (Contractor's default)

*Typical clauses*

(1) The Employer may forthwith determine the employment of the Contractor under this Agreement at any time giving written notice to the Contractor (provided that such notice shall not be given unreasonably or vexatiously) if the Contractor shall make default in any one or more of the following respects, that is to say:
   (a) if the Contractor without reasonable cause fails to proceed diligently with the Works or wholly suspends the carrying out of the Works before completion or fails within a reasonable time to comply with any instructions or variation ordered by the Architect/Supervising Officer;
   (b) if the Contractor becomes bankrupt or makes any composition or arrangement with his creditors or has a winding up order made or a resolution for voluntary winding up passed (except for the purposes of reconstruction) or a Receiver or Manager of his business is appointed or possession is taken by or on behalf of any creditor of any property the subject of a Charge.

Provided always that the right of determination shall be without prejudice to any other rights or remedies which the Employer may possess.

(2) In the event of the employment of the Contractor under this Contract being determined as aforesaid and so long as it has not been reinstated and continued, the following shall be the respective rights and duties of the Employer and Contractor:

    (a) the Employer may enter upon the Works and use all temporary buildings, plant, tools, equipment, goods and materials intended for, delivered to or placed on or adjacent to the Works;

    (b) the Contractor if so required by the Architect/Supervising Officer or Employer shall assign to the Employer without payment the benefit of any agreement for the supply of materials or goods and/or further execution of any work for the purpose of this Contract;

    (c) the Contractor shall allow or pay to the Employer the amount of any direct loss and/or damage caused to the Employer by the determination of such direct loss and/or damage being assessed by the Quantity Surveyor and certified by the Architect/Supervising Officer;

    (d) until after the completion of the Works the Employer shall not be bound to make any further payment to the Contractor but as soon as is reasonable thereafter the Architect/Supervising Officer shall issue a certificate showing the amount reported by the Quantity Surveyor as being due from the Employer or from the Contractor to the other whichever may be the case.

## 18. Determination by the Contractor

*Typical clauses*

(1) The Contractor may forthwith determine his employment under this Agreement at any time by giving written notice to the Employer in the event of one of the following:

    (a) the Quantity Surveyor failing to render reports as herein provided, or the Architect/Supervising Officer withholding the issue of a certificate and failing within seven days after notice in writing by the Contractor to issue such a certificate, or

    (b) the Employer not paying the Contractor any sum certified by the Architect/Supervising Officer within the time stated in Clause 14 and failing to make such a payment within seven days after receipt of notice from the Contractor of such non-payment, or

    (c) the Employer becoming bankrupt or making any composition or arrangement with his creditors, or

    (d) the Works being suspended for more than twenty-eight (28) days under the order of the Architect/Supervising Officer or any Court of Law or by the operation of any regulation of any competent authority or by reasons of, or resulting from legislation.

(2) In such case the Employer shall pay to the Contractor the amount specified in Clause 17(2) (a) and (b) and shall indemnify the Contractor against the liabilities specified in Clause 17(2)(c).

## 19. Non-assignment

*Typical clause*

Neither party shall assign any of its rights hereunder without the written consent of the other party, provided that the Contractor shall not unreasonably withhold his consent to the Employer assigning any of his rights.

## 20. Value Added Tax

*Typical clause*

The Employer shall reimburse the Contractor all payments, direct and indirect, made by the Contractor in connection with the Works in respect of Value Added Tax pursuant to the Finance Act 1972 or any amendment thereto and correctly chargeable to the Employer under this Contract and the Contractor shall obtain any necessary proof of payment by way of tax receipts or receipted invoices as the Employer, the Architect/Supervising Officer or the Quantity Surveyor may require.

## 21. Arbitration

*Typical clause*

Should any dispute or difference arise between the Employer (or the Architect/ Supervising Officer or the Quantity Surveyor on his behalf) and the Contractor in regard to matters controlled by this Agreement, such dispute or difference shall be referred to the arbitration and final decision of a person to be agreed between the parties or, failing agreement within fourteen (14) days' written notice asking for the appointment of an arbitrator being given by one party to the other, then, by a person appointed by the President of the Chartered Institute of Arbitrators upon request of either party.

**Signed on behalf of the Employer**

.................................................................................................

*Witness* ............................................................................................

Address ..............................................................................................

.................................................................................................

Occupation ........................................................................................

**Signed on behalf of the Contractor**

.................................................................................................

*Witness* ............................................................................................

Address ..............................................................................................

.................................................................................................

Occupation ........................................................................................

Date.....................................................................................................

## APPENDIX (A)

## DEFINITION OF PRIME COST

**Prime cost shall include:**

*Typical clauses*

(1) All payments made to or in connection with all persons engaged full or part-time upon the Works, including incentive payments, holiday stamps, bonus, general expenses, subsistence and travelling expenses, Employers' contributions to National Insurance and Government and Company Pensions Schemes and any payroll tax or other tax, levy, contribution or payment which may be imposed and which shall be payable by the Contractor in respect of such persons. The Contractor shall not be entitled without consultation with and the prior agreement of the Architect/ Supervising Officer to employ upon the Works any person whose normal place of employment or residence is unreasonably distant from the Works so as to incur travelling accommodation subsistence or other expenses which would not otherwise be incurred.

(2) The cost of materials and goods for incorporation in the Works and small tools not covered by the Working Rule Agreement, actually and necessarily used in connection with the Works.

(3) Payments due to sub-/works* contractors in accordance with the terms and conditions of their subcontract (after deduction of all discounts).

(4) The costs of statutory fees rates, taxes and charges incurred in compliance with Clause 6.

(5) Travelling and hotel accommodation and other expenses necessarily and unavoidably incurred by all the Contractor's site staff (salaried or otherwise) other than Directors unless previously specified prior to Contract.

(6) The cost of insuring against the responsibility of the Contractor under Clauses 15(3) and 16(2) and the cost of any other insurance effect on the instruction of the Employer.

(7) The cost of cartage, transport to and from site, erection, site maintenance and dismantling of plant, tools, scaffolding, sheds, mess rooms, etc. together with the running costs, i.e. electricity, gas, petrol, oil, etc. of all mechanical plant.

(8) The hire charge of the Contractor's own mechanical and non-mechanical plant at the scheduled rates agreed between the Contractor and the Quantity Surveyor and running and maintenance costs in connection therewith. The hire charge of other mechanical and non-mechanical plant at invoiced cost. Provided that in the opinion of the Quantity Surveyor such rates are competitive and that the plant is necessarily upon the site for the period so charged.

(9) All charges for rent, rates, Value Added Tax, other taxes telephone, stationery, office machinery and equipment, heating, lighting, cleaning and all other expenditure relating to site accommodation and the site.

* Delete where applicable.

(10) The cost of any tax, levy, contribution or payment or of any variation in tax legislation which may be imposed and which shall be payable by the Contractor in respect of the Works.

(11) All costs referred to in this Appendix shall be net after the deduction of:
  (a) Trade and cash discounts.
  (b) Sales or transfers of old or new materials or plant.
  (c) Any other commission, off-set and the like properly paid or allowed to the Contractor in connection with cost described herein.

(12) Deduction of credits for sums ascertained under Clauses 7 and 9.

## APPENDIX (B)

## THE MANAGEMENT FEE

### The management fee shall include:

*Typical clauses*

(1) The management, organizational, accounting and specialist services of Head and Regional Head Office staff.

(2) The cost of keeping proper accounts on the Contractor's normal Costing System and providing facilities for checking the Prime Cost by the Quantity Surveyor and the Supervising Officer.

(3) All charges for rent, rates, taxes, telephone, stationery, heating, lighting, cleaning and all other overhead expenditure relating to the Contractor's Head and Regional Head Offices.

(4) All expenses incurred by Directors, including the cost of travelling and hotel accommodation except those specified prior to Contract.

(5) Profit.

### Schedule

Situation of the Works:

Employer:

Contractor:

Architect/Supervising Officer:

Quantity Surveyor:

Liquidated Damages:                    £                    per week.

Estimate of Prime Cost:

Date of Possession:

Date of Completion:                    As Time and Progress Schedule

Management Fee:                    % of the Final Adjusted Estimate of Prime Cost.

# Appendix B

---

## Typical example of duties and responsibilities of the parties for inclusion in tender documents

---

# TYPICAL EXAMPLE OF DUTIES AND RESPONSIBILITIES OF THE PARTIES

## Preconstruction period

### Generally

The following lists, which shall not be regarded as exhaustive, are provided to amplify the Duties and Responsibilities of the Parties as envisaged under the Contract.

### Employer

(1) Agreement of brief with Architect.
(2) Approve design submitted by the Architect and any changes thereto.
(3) Establish and agree the financial limitation for completing the Works.
(4) Approve and give financial sanction to preordering or purchasing of materials, plant and labour during the preconstruction period.
(5) Give possession of the site to Managing Contractor.

### Architect

(1) Confirm design matters with Employer.
(2) Establish total budget available for project and advise Employer of compatability with design brief.
(3) Design and design co-ordination including establishing final briefs for structural, mechanical and electrical consultants.
(4) Agree subcontract documentation with Quantity Surveyor.
(5) Approve and agree all programmes.
(6) Approve and agree with Managing Contractor the extent of pre-ordering or purchasing, materials, plant and labour. Inspect and approve items purchased.
(7) Compile tender lists in conjunction with Quantity Surveyor and Managing Contractor. Provide subcontract tender documents. Appoint subcontractor.
(8) Issue all instructions necessary for commencement of the Works.

### Quantity Surveyor

(1) Prepare initial Cost Plan based on agreed Estimate of Prime Cost.
(2) Monitor and adjust Cost Plan.
(3) Prepare subcontract documentation, including Agreement, Terms and Conditions and Warranty agreement, and agree same with the Architect and Managing Contractor.
(4) Provide tender documents for work to be subcontracted.

(5)  Check and report on subcontracted tenders and make recommendation to Architect.

## Contractor

(1)  Advise Architect on drawing programme to meet the needs of the construction programme.
(2)  Advise Architect on availability and costs of materials to be used including alternatives when necessary.
(3)  Advise Architect as to most economical construction methods, sequences, materials and specialist installations to enable the constructional elements to be broken down into tenderable work packages.
(4)  Provide Architect with a programme for constructing the Works, illustrating the various work packages, the interrelationship between design activities, tendering, purchasing, construction, and completion of each major element. The programme is to be updated on four week cycles throughout the preconstruction period and supported by schedules listing critical dates for commencement or completion of the various activities shown.
(5)  Assist Quantity Surveyor in preparation of an initial Cost Plan and assist in continual updating as design develops.
(6)  Advise Architect from time to time on the basis of information available when construction can commence on site.
(7)  Advise Architect of suitable subcontractors for the work packages and make recommendations on basis of discreet investigations as to their current capability and financial stability.
(8)  Advise Quantity Surveyor on form of tender, subcontract agreement, Terms and Conditions, design warranty, performance bond, the facilities and attendances which are to be provided for the subcontractors.
(9)  Provide Architect with a site layout, showing extent of site required, position of hoardings, fans, fences, hoists, gantries, scaffolding, position and capacity of communal plant, office accommodation, welfare facilities, compound areas, temporary services, etc.
(10)  Provide Architect with details of all labour, materials and plant which are required to be pre-ordered or purchased prior to the construction period to enable the Works to be completed without delay and advise on financial commitments as they are incurred. Approval (in writing) of Architect must be obtained before placing orders.
(11)  Attend such meetings as may be necessary or required by Architect to ensure that design work is proceeding in a satisfactory manner in accordance with the programme.

# SCHEDULE OF PERSONNEL

## Preconstruction period

The Contractor shall list here the staff he will assign to the project during preconstruction period giving details of their duties and responsibilities.

STATUS/TITLE     NAME IF KNOWN        Duties and responsibilities

The Contractor shall submit with his tender a chart showing lines of responsibility.

## Construction period

*Generally*

The following lists, which shall not be regarded as exhaustive, indicate the Duties and Responsibilities of the Parties.

## Employer

(a) Continue the responsibilities undertaken during the Preconstruction Period insofar as they apply to the Construction Period.
(b) Authorize additional monies for 'Brief' changes required by the Employer.
(c) Payment of Interim and Final Certificates, Management and Consultants' fees, all valid claims agreed by Architect.
(d) Arrange Employer/Consultant meetings.

## Architect

(a) Continue the responsibilities undertaken during the Preconstruction Period insofar as they apply to the Construction Period.
(b) Provide all drawings and specifications as required to construct the Works.
(c) Compile tender lists in conjunction with Quantity Surveyor and Managing Contractor. Issue instructions to appoint subcontractors.
(d) Issue all instructions necessary for carrying out the Works.
(e) Monitor the Managing Contractor's site operations.
(f) Set standards and approve final quality of all materials and workmanship incorporated in the Works.
(g) Review details and specifications from time to time to ensure Final Cost does not exceed budget provided for scheme.
(h) Issue certificates and submit to Employer for payment.
(i) Compile list and ensure all defects are made good.

## Quantity Surveyor

(a) Continue the responsibilities undertaken during the Preconstruction Period insofar as they apply to the Construction Period.
(b) Update Cost Plan by replacing estimated figures with actual costs as and when they occur and report to Architect.
(c) Report Costs to Employer and Design Team regularly.
(d) Advise Architect of any savings or overexpenditure as they become known.
(e) Provide monthly reports to enable Architect to issue interim certificates.
(f) Prepare Final Adjusted Estimate of Prime Cost.
(g) Provide Employer with Final Cost Statement.
(h) Provide the Contractor with any 'Bills of Quantities' agreed between the Quantity Surveyor and the Contractor as necessary in respect of any part or parts of the Works to be subcontracted by the Contractor.

## Contractor

(a) Continue the responsibilities undertaken during the Preconstruction Period insofar as they apply to the Construction Period.

(b) Take possession of site and provide temporary office accommodation, canteens, sanitary accommodations, stores, drying rooms, workshops, compounds, protective fencing, etc. for his own use, also Architect's and subcontractor's site meetings.

(c) Provide all necessary information to enable Quantity Surveyor to value the Works.

(d) Enter into subcontract agreements, supervise and co-ordinate all subcontract work and ensure that any subcontractors' drawings are submitted in time to avoid causing delay.

(e) Co-ordinate and execute the Works.

(f) Initiate and attend subcontractors' meetings.

(g) Attend Architect and Consultant meetings.

(h) Make payments to subcontractors and Suppliers and agree all accounts with Quantity Surveyor.

(i) Make good all defects as listed by Architect.

(j) Advise Architect and Quantity Surveyor of any foreseeable or potential claim situation and recommend course of action required to avoid such claims.

(k) Monitor building programme and adjust target dates, notify all affected parties and advise Consultants of final completion date.

(l) Assist Quantity Surveyor to prepare Final Adjusted Estimate of Prime Cost.

(m) Agree Final Adjusted Estimate of Prime Cost and provide Quantity Surveyor with a 'No Further Claims' certificate.

(n) Provide each week for the Architect and Quantity Surveyor a daily labour record showing the number and description of tradesmen and labourers employed on the Works, including those employed by subcontractors.

(o) Provide each month for the Architect and Quantity Surveyor a daily labour record showing the number and titles of site management staff together with a record of persons visiting the site.

(p) Provide each week for the Architect and Quantity Surveyor a daily plant record showing the number, type and capacity of all plant excluding hand tools, currently employed on the Works. The time at which plant arrives on or departs from the site shall be recorded.

(q) Keep and make available to the Architect when required to do so a record of climatic conditions showing daily maximum and minimum air temperatures (including overnight) and the number of hours during the working day in which work is prevented by inclement weather.

(r) Take adequate precautions against nuisance and pollution from smoke, dust, rubbish, noise and other causes.

(s) Take all necessary precautions to prevent any trespass on adjoining property by men, plant or materials.

(t) Take adequate precautions to prevent personal injury, death and damage from fire.

(u) Take adequate precautions to prevent personal injury to persons having access to the site.

(v) Indemnify the Employer against any claim or action for damage from trespass or other nuisance.

The Contractor shall list here the staff he will assign to the project during the Construction Period giving details of their duties and responsibilities.

STATUS/TITLE       NAME IF KNOWN        Duties and responsibilities

The Contractor shall submit with his tender a chart showing lines of responsibility, and shall indicate if personnel are expected to carry out their duties at the Contractor's Head Office, Regional Office or on site.

# *Appendix C*

---

# Typical work-parcel form of contract

---

(See explanatory note on page 28)

SUBCONTRACT

for

CONTRACT FOR

.................................................

at

.................................................

PARCEL ........................................................   No...........................................

..............MANAGEMENT CONTRACTING LIMITED

Subcontract No................

THIS SUBCONTRACT is made the ..................................... day of ....................
19          BETWEEN ............. MANAGEMENT CONTRACTING LIMITED OF
                              (hereinafter called 'the Contractor' of the one part)
and ...........................................................................................................................
.................................................................................................................................
of or whose registered office is situated at ..............................................................
.................................................................................................................................
(hereinafter called 'the Subcontractor' of the other part).

WHEREAS by an Agreement (hereinafter referred to as 'the Management
Contract') made the ......................... day of ..................................... 19
between .................................................................................... of the one part
(hereinafter called 'the Employer' and the Contractor of the other part, the
Contractor undertook to manage organize secure and supervise the carrying
out and completion of the .........................................................................................
.............................................................................. (hereinafter referred to as the
Main Contract Works).

AND WHEREAS the Contractor desires to have executed the works of which
particulars are set out in Section B Part 1 of the Appendix to this Subcontract
(hereinafter referred to as 'the Subcontract Works') and which form part of the
Main Contract Works comprised in and to be executed in accordance with the
Management Contract, and any authorized variations of the Subcontract
Works;

AND WHEREAS the Management Contract requires that the Contractor shall
not employ any Subcontractor who will not enter into this

*(A)  The Subcontractor is the user of the current Subcontractor's tax certificate
      under the provisions of the Finance (Nr 2) Act 1975 (hereinafter called 'the
      Act') in one of the forms specified in Regulation 15 of the Income Tax
      (Sub-Contractors in the Construction Industry) Regulations, 1975 and the
      Schedule thereto (hereinafter called 'the Regulations').
*(B)  The Subcontractor is not the user of a current Subcontractor's tax
      certificate under the provisions of the Finance (Nr 2) Act 1975 (hereinafter
      called 'the Act') in one of the forms specified in Regulation 15 of the
      Income Tax (Sub-Contractors in the Construction Industry) Regulations
      1975 and the Schedule thereto (hereinafter called 'the Regulations').
 (C)  The Contractor is the user of a current Subcontractor's tax certificate under
      the Act and the Regulations.
 (D)  The Employer under the Management Contract is a Contractor within the
      meaning of the Act and the Regulations.

* Delete whichever alternative is not applicable.

NOW IT IS HEREBY AGREED AND DECLARED that the Subcontractor shall carry out and complete the Subcontract Works in accordance with, and the rights and duties of the Contractor and the Subcontractor shall be regulated by:

(a) Clauses 1 to 24 inclusive of the NFBTE/FASS Sub-Contract Form 'for use where the Sub-Contractor is nominated under the 1963 edition of the Standard Form of Building Contract issued by the Joint Contracts Tribunal' (revised April 1978).

(b) Amendments to the aforementioned Clauses 1 to 24 as set out in Appendix A Part 1 to this Subcontract.

(c) Additional Clauses 25 to 30 inclusive as set out in Appendix A Part 2 to this Subcontract.

AND it is further agreed that for the operation of this Subcontract but no further or otherwise all reference to the Main Contract shall be deemed to be a reference to the Standard Form of Building Contract with Quantities Local Authorities Edition 1963 (July 1977 revision) incorporating Amendment No. 15/1978. Details of the conditions of this 'deemed to be' Main Contract including amendments thereto are set out in Appendix C to this Subcontract and such conditions will apply to the operation of this Subcontract unless amended by the terms and conditions of the Management Contract in which case the latter will take precedence.

IN WITNESS WHEREOF the parties hereto have hereunto set their hands the day and year first above written:

Signed by the above named Contractor in the presence of

.................................................................

.................................................................

................................................
MANAGEMENT
CONTRACTING LTD

Signed by the above named Subcontrac-tor in the presence of

.................................................................

.................................................................

................................................

## APPENDIX A

## Part I

Amendments to Clauses 1 to 24 of the NFBTE/FASS Sub-Contract Form.

Clauses 1 to 24 of the aforementioned Sub-Contract Form shall be deemed to be amended as follows.

### Generally

Notwithstanding the title of the above mentioned Sub-Contract Form the Sub-Contractor is not 'nominated'.

All references to 'Appendix to this Sub-Contract' shall read 'Appendix B to this Sub-Contract'.
All references to 'Architect' shall mean 'Supervising Officer'.
All references to 'Contractor' shall mean 'Management Contractor'.

**Clause 1.** INSERT after Main Contract the words 'and the Management Contract'.

**Clause 4.** ADD to end of clause . . . 'without prejudice to the indemnities contained in Clause 3(b) of this Sub-Contract the insurances to be maintained by the Sub-Contractor shall have a limit of indemnity of not less than £     for any one occurrence and shall be unlimited as to the number of occurrences'.

### Completion

**Clause 8   Sub-Clause (a).** The first paragraph is to be deleted and the following substituted:
'The Sub-Contractor shall commence the Sub-Contract Works upon receipt in writing from the Contractor of the requisite notice to commence as stated in Part II Section B of the Appendix to this Sub-Contract and shall proceed with the same with due expedition'.

**Clause 8   Sub-Clause (a).** Delete the fourth paragraph as follows 'Provided that the . . . as the case may be'.

Insert new Sub-Clause (c) (iv) as follows:
**Clause 8   Sub-Clause (c) (iv).** 'Any breach by the Sub-Contractor of the Conditions of this Sub-Contract which affects the completion of the Main Contract Works may result in loss and/or expense being incurred by the Employer and the Sub-Contractor hereby acknowledges that such loss and/or expense is in the contemplation of the parties and accepts that he is liable to the Contractor for payment of such loss and/or expense which is the result of such breach. The Sub-Contractor is advised that the Employer has calculated the loss and/or expense which he will incur in the Main Contract Works or any specified section thereof are not available to him by the Date or Dates for Completion and has expressed these amounts as liquidated and ascertained damages and these are stated in the tender documents.'

### Value Added Tax

Delete Clause 10A.

**Finance Act**

*Delete Clause 10C.

or

*Delete Clause 10D and Clauses 10C(3)(a) and (b) and substitute the following:

10C(3) (a)   Where the tax certificate produced to the Contractor is in one of the forms numbered 714I or 714P in the Schedule to the Regulations the Sub-Contractor is relieved of the obligation under Regulation 23(1) of the Regulations of giving the Contractor vouchers (Forms 715) for every payment he receives from the Contractor from which the deduction has not been referred to in S.69(4) of the Act. Instead the Sub-Contractor shall supply one voucher only at the start of each Sub-Contract.

10C(3) (b)   The Contractor shall pass the voucher referred to in paragraph (a) of this sub-clause to the Inland Revenue.

10C(3) (c)   The special provisions in paragraphs (a) and (b) of this sub-clause are in accordance with undertakings given by the Contractor to the Inland Revenue and in accordance with the letter of Authorization from the Inland Revenue dated 20th July 1976 ref. 271/8475/RGE, a copy of which is available from the Contractor.

**Interim Payment**

Delete Sub-Clause 11(b) (ii) and the words from Sub-Clause 11(c) 'less a cash discount of 2½% if payment is made within 14 days of the receipt by the contractor of that certificate or duplicate copy thereof'.

**Dispute as to Certificate**

Delete Sub-Clause 11(d).

**Special Interim Payment**

Delete Sub-Clause 11(f).

**Provision of Water Etc.**

In Clause 16 delete Sub-Clause (a) and substitute as follows:

(a) The Contractor will provide the services and attendances detailed in the General Conditions of the Tender Document. Subject as aforesaid the Sub-Contractor shall make all other necessary provisions in regard to the said matters.

* Delete whichever alternative is not applicable.

## Fluctuations

*Clause 23A, C D & E shall apply.
*Clause 23B, C D & E shall apply.
*Clause 23F shall apply.
*Delete Clause 23.

## Arbitration

In Clause 24 insert in the fourth paragraph after the phrase 'Arbitration Act 1950 (notwithstanding anything in Section 34 thereof) . . .' and of the Arbitration Act 1979) shall . . .

# Part II

Additional Clauses to the NFBTE/FASS Sub-Contract Form.

## Clause 25   Execution

This Sub-Contract shall be deemed for the purposes only of the Limitation Act 1939 to be executed under seal and neither party shall assert in any action or arbitration, or otherwise rely on, any shorter period of limitation than is prescribed by that Act for contracts under seal.

## Clause 26   Retention of Title

The Sub-Contractor shall wherever possible ensure that goods and materials delivered to the Site for incorporation in the Sub-Contract Works, are the property of the Sub-Contractor. Where such goods and materials are not the property of the Sub-Contractor the Contractor shall be notified in writing:

(a) That this is the case.
(b) When they became the property of the Sub-Contractor.

## †Clause 27   Warranty

The Sub-Contractor shall execute in favour of the Employer a warranty against default or negligence in the design and/or selection of materials.

---

\* Delete whichever alternatives are not applicable.
† Delete as appropriate.

### Clause 28   Strikes — Loss and/or Expense

If the Main Contract Works or the Sub-Contract Works are affected by a local combination of workmen, strike or lockout affecting any of the trades employed upon the Works or any of the trades engaged in the preparation manufacture of transportation of any of the goods or materials required for the Work:

(i)   Neither the Contractor nor the Sub-Contractor shall be entitled to make any claim upon the other, for any loss and/or expense resulting from such action as aforesaid.
(ii)  The Contractor shall take all reasonable practicable steps to keep the site open and available for the use of the Sub-Contractor.
(iii) The Sub-Contractor shall take all reasonable practicable steps to continue with the Sub-Contract Works.

Nothing in this clause shall affect any other right of the Contractor or the Sub-Contractor under this Sub-Contract if such action as aforesaid occurs.

### Clause 29   Bond

It is a requirement that prior to the acceptance of a tender for this Sub-Contract Work, the Tenderer shall provide a Bond to the value of 10% of the Sub-Contract sum from an approved surety in favour of the Management Contract.

### Clause 30   Incorporated Documents

It is hereby agreed that this Sub-Contract incorporates the provisions and/or agreements contained in the following documents and it shall be construed as if the same had been set out herein at length:

## APPENDIX B

## Part I

**Second Recital**     Particulars of the Works (being a part of the Works comprised in the Main Contract in this Sub-Contract referred to as 'the Sub-Contract Works'), viz:

.........................................................................................

.........................................................................................

.........................................................................................

.........................................................................................

## Part II

**Clause 8**

Description of work          Completion period or periods of the Sub-Contract Works or respective sections thereof

...............................................................................................
...............................................................................................
...............................................................................................
...............................................................................................
...............................................................................................
...............................................................................................
...............................................................................................
...............................................................................................
...............................................................................................
...............................................................................................
...............................................................................................
...............................................................................................
...............................................................................................
...............................................................................................

Period of Notice to commence Sub-Contract Works – Clause 8(a)

.................... weeks

## Part III

**Clause 10**

Value of the Sub-Contract Works

...............................................................................................
...............................................................................................
...............................................................................................
...............................................................£

## Part IIIA

**Clause 10(b) (3) (A) or (B)**

Percentage Additions on Prime Cost of Daywork Calculated in accordance with the definition of prime cost of daywork issued by the Royal Institution of Chartered Surveyors and the

...............................................................................................
(i)    Labour ..................................................... %
(ii)   Materials ................................................. %
(iii)  Plant......................................................... %

## Part IV

**Clause 11**

Retention Percentage............................5.........................%
(*Note* – The percentage of payments to be retained by the
Contractor should be stated, this should not exceed the
Retention Percentage under the Main Contract.)

## Part V

**Clause 23A(c) (i)**

List of Basic Prices

...................................................................................................
...................................................................................................
...................................................................................................
...................................................................................................
...................................................................................................
...................................................................................................
...................................................................................................
...................................................................................................
...................................................................................................
...................................................................................................

## Part VI

**Clause 23B(b) (i)**

List of Materials and Goods

...................................................................................................
...................................................................................................
...................................................................................................
...................................................................................................
...................................................................................................
...................................................................................................

## Part VII

**Clause 23D (6)**

Date of Tender
The date of tender is the ............. day of ............... 19..........

## Part VIII

**Clause 23E**

Percentage Addition on Fluctuations.............Nil.............%

## Part IX

**Clause 23F(1)**

The Nominated Sub-Contract Formula Rules are those
dated .............................................................................................
.........................................................................19..........

## Part X

Clause 23F(3) (iii)
and (3) (iv)

Non-Adjustable Element.................................................. %
(Not to exceed 10%)
(*Note* – Only applicable where the Main Contract is let on the Standard Form of Building Contract, Edition,        ; Quantities.)

## Part XI

Clause 23F(4)

List of Market Prices

........................................................................................
........................................................................................
........................................................................................
........................................................................................
........................................................................................
........................................................................................
........................................................................................

## Part XII

Nominated Sub-Contract Formula Rules

Rule 1

Part 1 only: Balance of Adjustable Work; any measured work not allocated to a Work Category

........................................................................................
........................................................................................
........................................................................................
........................................................................................
........................................................................................

Base month ..........................................................................
Date of Tender .....................................................................

Rule 11(b)

Part 1 only: the Work Categories applicable to the Sub-Contract Works

........................................................................................
........................................................................................
........................................................................................
........................................................................................
........................................................................................

Rule 15

Method of dealing with 'Fix-only' work

........................................................................................
........................................................................................
........................................................................................
........................................................................................
........................................................................................

| | |
|---|---|
| **Rule 26** | Part II only: Weightings of Labour and materials – Electrical Installations |
| | Labour................................................................................ % |
| | Materials............................................................................ % |
| | Heating, Ventilation and Air Conditioning Installations |
| | Labour................................................................................ % |
| | Materials............................................................................ % |

**Rule 40**    Part II only: Lift Installations – Element of Sub-Contract Sum
subject to formula adjustment

..........................................................................................

..........................................................................................

..........................................................................................

**Rule 45**    Part II only: Structural Steelwork Installations:
(i)    Average price per tonne of steel delivered to fabrica-
tor's works
£........................................................................

(ii)    Average price per tonne for erection of steelwork
£........................................................................

**Rule 51**    Part II only: Catering Equipment Installations:
Apportionment of values –
(i)    Materials and shop fabrication....................................
(ii)    Supply of factor items..................................................
(iii)    Site installation............................................................

## Part XIII

**Clause 13B(1) (b)**    Adjudicator............................................................................
**Clause 13B(4) (a)**    Trustee -Stakeholder..............................................................

..........................................................................................

..........................................................................................

## APPENDIX C

## Details of main contract

A. The Management Contract has been specially prepared for this Project, but
for the operation of this Sub-Contract the Main Contract shall be deemed to
be the Standard Form of Building Contract Local Authorities Edition with
Quantities 1963 Edition (July 1977 Revision) incorporating Amendment No.
15/1978 issued January 1978.

Clause 1–11        As standard form.
Clause 12        Contract Bills

|  | Delete '5th edition Imperial revised 1964/5th edition Metric' and insert '6th edition'. |
|---|---|
| Clause 13–16 | As standard form. |
| Clause 17 | As standard form. |
| Clause 18–19 | As standard form. |
| Clause 20 | Delete alterations (A) and (B). |
| Clause 21–26 | As standard form. |
| Clause 27–28 | Delete entirely. |
| Clause 29–35 | As standard form. |

Appendix to Main Contract

| Clause 15, 16 and 30 | Defects Liability Period |
|---|---|
|  | Building –    months |
|  | Services Installation –    months. |
| Clause 19(1) | Insurance Cover – £    million. |
| Clause 21 | Date for Possession———. |
|  | Date for Completion———. |
| Clause 22 | Liquidated and Ascertained Damages – £    per week. |
| Clause 26 | Period of Delay –    months. |
| Clause 30(1) | Period of Interim Certificates –    month(s). |
| Clause 30(3) | Retention Percentage –    %. |
| Clause 30(5) | Period of Final Measure –    months. |
| Clause 30(6) | Period for issue of Final Certificate –    months. |

# *Appendix D*

## Budgetary control system – complete set of forms

FINANCIAL STATEMENT

CONTRACT:

for

EMPLOYER

REPORT
No: _____          DATE: _____

£          £          £

1.  CONTRACT EPC AND
    MANAGEMENT FEE

    AUTHORIZED EXTRAS/SAVINGS

    TOTAL AUTHORIZED EPC
    AND MANAGEMENT FEE

2.  PROJECTED FINAL COST

3.  Less   FLUCTUATIONS

4.  Less   OTHER ADJUSTMENTS

           ADJUSTED EPC
           (including contingencies)
           (excluding  fluctuations)

5.  Add    MANAGEMENT FEE
           (calculated on above
           Adjusted EPC)

6.  PROJECTED FINAL COST
    AND MANAGEMENT FEE
    (excluding fluctuations)

7.  ESTIMATED OVER/(UNDER)
    SPEND

8.  ALLOWANCE FOR
    FLUCTUATIONS From Line 3 £
       Add Management Fee (     ) £

9.  PROJECTED FINAL COST
    AND MANAGEMENT FEE
    INCLUDING FLUCTUATIONS

Signed ..........................
        DEARLE AND HENDERSON
        Chartered Quantity Surveyors

**Form 1** Financial statement.

CONTRACT: _____ JOB NO: _____

SUMMARY OF PROJECTED/FINAL COST: _____ FINANCIAL REPORT NO: _____ DATE: _____ SHEET 1

| WORK PARCEL | | CONTRACT EFC £ | PROJECTED FINAL COST £ | CONTAINED WITHIN PROJECTED FINAL COST | | | | REMARKS |
|---|---|---|---|---|---|---|---|---|
| No: | Title | | | FLUCTUATIONS £ | EFC ADJUSTMENTS £ | OTHER ADJUSTMENTS £ | CONTINGENCY £ | |
| | | | | | | | | |
| C/FWD | | | | | | | | |

Form 2, sheet 1   Summary of projected/final cost

| CONTRACT: | | | | | | | | | JOB NO: |
|---|---|---|---|---|---|---|---|---|---|
| SUMMARY OF PROJECTED/FINAL COST: | | FINANCIAL REPORT NO: | | DATE: | | | | | SHEET 2 |
| WORK PARCEL | | CONTRACT EPC £ | PROJECTED FINAL COST £ | CONTAINED WITHIN PROJECTED FINAL COST: | | | | REMARKS | |
| No: | Title | | | FLUCTUATIONS £ | EPC ADJUSTMENTS £ | OTHER ADJUSTMENTS £ | CONTINGENCY £ | | |
| | B/Fwd | | | | | | | | |
| | | | | | | | | | |
| Sub-total (excluding contract contingencies) | | | | | | | | | |
| Contract Contingencies | | | | | | | | | |
| TOTALS | | | | | | | | | |

Form 2, sheet 2

PROJECTED/FINAL COST RECORD SHEET

WORK PARCEL REF

SUB PARCEL REF

CONTRACT
JOB NO:

| | A | B |
|---|---|---|
| | £ | £ |

1. CONTRACT EPC

   A. Cost reimbursable allocation

   B. Fixed-price allocation

2. ESTIMATED VALUE OF A/SO INSTRUCTIONS

| A/SO/1 No | Classification | | | | |
|---|---|---|---|---|---|
| | Non-EPC | Adj EPC | | | |
| | | | A | B | A | B |
| | £ | £ | £ | £ |
| | | | | | |
| C/Fwd | | | | | |

2. CON'T

| A/SO/1 No: | Classifications | | | | |
|---|---|---|---|---|---|
| | Non-EPC | Adj EPC | | | |
| | | | A | B | A | B |
| | £ | £ | £ | £ |
| B/FWD | | | | | |

ADJUSTED EPC

3. OTHER ADJUSTMENTS

| | A | B |
|---|---|---|
| | £ | £ |

4. FLUCTUATIONS

5. CONTINGENCY

| | A | B |
|---|---|---|
| | £ | £ |

PROJECTED/FINAL COST

Form 3  Projected/final cost record sheet.

CONTRACT:     JOB NO:

PROJECTED/FINAL COST COLLECTION SHEET     WORK PARCEL REF:

FINANCIAL REPORT NO:     DATE:

| SUB-PARCEL REF: | CONTRACT EPC | PROJECTED FINAL COST £ | CONTAINED WITHIN PROJECTED FINAL COST | | | |
|---|---|---|---|---|---|---|
| | | | FLUCTUATIONS £ | EPC ADJUSTMENTS £ | OTHER ADJUSTMENTS £ | CONTINGENCY £ |
| | | | | | | |
| TO SUMMARY OF PROJECTED FINAL COST | | | | | | |

**Form 4** Projected/final cost collection sheet.

```
(SUB) PARCEL RECONCILIATION SHEET (1)

CONTRACT:                                              JOB NO:


PARCEL REF:

                                                            £

ACCEPTED TENDER (Exclusive of cash discount) .........

Deduct Contingencies and Dayworks ....................


                                                    _____

                      Balance ...........

CONTRACT EPC .......................................
                                                    _____

                      Amount of Accepted Tender
                      Above/below Contract EPC

                                                    _____


Value/Assessment of Fluctuations
contained in Accepted Tender                    £
                                                    _____

Value of items contained in amount of
Accepted Tender above/below Contract
EPC that will not be included in Final
Adjusted EPC                                    £

Brief Description        £
                      + or (-)



                    _____        Less      _____
Non-EPC Adj.                           Adj. EPC

                    _____                  _____
```

**Form 5, sheet 1**   (Sub-)Contract parcel reconciliation sheet.

(SUB) PARCEL RECONCILIATION SHEET (2)

List of Provisional Sums contained in tender
(other than Contingencies and Dayworks)

| Ref | Description | Amount £ |
|-----|-------------|----------|
|     |             |          |

**Form 5, sheet 2**

| APPLICATION NO: | DATE | LABOUR £ | MATERIALS £ | PLANT £ | TOTAL £ | FLUCTUATIONS INCLUDED IN TOTAL £ | TOTAL £ | FLUCTUATIONS £ |
|---|---|---|---|---|---|---|---|---|
| | | | | | | | RUNNING TOTALS | |
| | | | | | | | | |
| | | | | | | | | |
| TOTALS | | | | | | | | |

ACCOUNTING RECORD SHEET – COST REIMBURSABLE

CONTRACT:

PARCEL REF:

CONTRACTOR:

JOB NO:

Form 6   Accounting sheet, cost reimbursable.

| EXPENDITURE REVIEW: | | JOB NO: |
|---|---|---|
| CONTRACT: | PARCEL REF: | |

| SECTION | PROGRESS   APPLICATION NO: | | | |
|---|---|---|---|---|
| | | | DATE: | |
| | LABOUR £ | MATERIALS £ | PLANT £ | TOTAL £ |
| A.    COST REIMBURSABLE | | | | |
| B/Fwd. From Previous Applications | | | | |
| This application: | | | | |
| (i) | | | | |
| (ii) | | | | |
| B.    GENERAL USE MATERIALS (Value allocated) | | | | |
| C.    FIXED PRICE CONTRACTS | | | | |
| (i) | | | | |
| (ii) | | | | |
| | TOTAL EXPENDITURE COMMITTED | | | |
| | LATEST PROJECTED FINAL COST | | | |
| | BALANCE AVAILABLE FOR REMAINDER OF WORK | | | |
| FINANCIAL REPORT NO: | | | | |

**Form 7**  Expenditure review.

| CONTRACT : | | | JOB NO: |
|---|---|---|---|
| SUMMARY OF GENERAL USE MATERIALS | | | |
| APPLICATION NR: | DATE | VALUE £ | COMMENTS |
| | | | |

**Form 8**   General-use materials record.

QUANTITY SURVEYORS REPORT   SHEET 1

VALUATION No.      for _____

Works

Employer

Architect/
Supervising
Officer

Management
Contractor

|  | Contract Value £ | Fluctuations £ | Total £ |
|---|---|---|---|
| Management Contractors Work Parcel Contractors Work |  |  |  |
| Sub-Total |  |  |  |
| Management Fee    % on £ |  |  |  |
| Total Carried Forward |  |  |  |

**Form 9, sheet 1**   Quantity surveyor's report, valuation.

```
CONTRACT:                                    QUANTITY SURVEYORS
                                             REPORT SHEET 2




Valuation No.        for                                              £


              Total brought forward

Less Retention

     Parcel Contractors       % on £

     Management Fee           % on £       _____




Deduct   release of rentention on issue
 of certificates of practical completion
and/or making good defects


     Parcel Contractors
     Management Fee          _____    _____    _____

     TOTAL DUE TO DATE

     Less Amount Previously Certified                    _____


     BALANCE RECOMMENDED FOR PAYMENT            £        _____
                                                         ==========




        .......................... DEARLE AND HENDERSON
                          Chartered Quantity Surveyors
```

**Form 9, sheet 2**

# Index